1495

THE WIDE, WIDE CIRCLE
OF DIVINE LOVE

Other books by W. Eugene March
by Presbyterian Publishing Corp.

Israel and the Politics of Land: A Theological Case Study (Westminster John Knox Press)

The Mighty Acts of God by Arnold B. Rhodes, revised by W. Eugene March (Geneva Press)

THE WIDE, WIDE CIRCLE
OF DIVINE LOVE

A BIBLICAL CASE FOR
RELIGIOUS DIVERSITY

W. Eugene March

WESTMINSTER
JOHN KNOX PRESS
LOUISVILLE · KENTUCKY

Book design by Sharon Adams
Cover design by Pam Poll Graphic Design
Cover art © Corbis

First edition
Published by Westminster John Knox Press
Louisville, Kentucky

This book is printed on acid-free paper that meets the American National Standards Institute Z39.48 standard. ♾

PRINTED IN THE UNITED STATES OF AMERICA

05 06 07 08 09 10 11 12 13 14 — 10 9 8 7 6 5 4 3 2 1

Library of Congress Cataloging-in-Publication Data

March, W. Eugene (Wallace Eugene), 1935–
    The wide, wide circle of divine love : a biblical case for religious diversity / W. Eugene March. — 1st ed.
        p. cm.
    ISBN 0-664-22708-2 (alk. paper)
        1. Christianity and other religions. 2. Religious pluralism—Christianity. 3. Christianity and other religions—Biblical teaching. 4. Religious pluralism—Christianity—Biblical teaching. I. Title.

BR127.M28 2005
261.2—dc22

                                            2004050882

To Margaret
Encouraging Friend, Beloved Wife

Contents

Preface

This book was not prompted by the horrendous events of September 11, 2001, but new impetus was certainly given as that reality began to shape perception and reflection. The book actually began, at least in my inner being, forty years ago as a result of studying under the tutelage of several Jewish professors and in the company of Jewish students in New York City. As I encountered these people as people, and particularly as people of deep religious commitment, I was compelled to understand them in a new way. They were every bit as committed to the service of God as was I. But if Jesus was the Way, the Truth, and the Life, as I believed, what were these folks up to? If one could only know the "Father" through Jesus Christ, how could I understand the clear reflection of God's way "enfleshed" by these people? This initiated a journey of interfaith exploration that has continued down to the present and has been more valuable to me than words can express.

My personal journey and involvements have led me into rigorous and rich interaction not only with Jews but also, though to a lesser degree, with Muslims, Buddhists, and Hindus. This involvement was propelled, at least in part, by the disconnect between my official theology and my unofficial experience of others. My deep allegiance to Jesus Christ (one that continues to direct and sustain me) seemed to discredit or deny the experience and commitments of others. How could the One whom I knew as the Way, the Truth, and the Life have disdain for or reject the wonderful people I was working with? It simply did not compute.

Therein began a long pilgrimage of studying and wrestling with the Bible in connection with these matters. The journey was assisted by serious interfaith dialogue with a number of people. The more I studied the Bible and the more I tried to understand and share my own faith, the clearer the conviction became that discipleship to Jesus invited a person into a very wide circle of people for whom God cares. Jesus is God's love incarnate, and that love embraces the world. The particularity of incarnate love requires reflection on the messiness of human communities, within and beyond the church, but it does not necessitate the rejection of all other particular experiences of divine grace. Because I was claimed by Jesus Christ, I was impelled to find ways to understand and love others, especially others who on the surface seem to have a rather different worldview.

My experience leads me to the conviction that the practice of love, not the defense of doctrine, is the primary challenge for Christians (and adherents of other religious traditions as well) in today's world. The truth of Jesus' way that leads to life is the participation in God's love that the Bible declares is extended to all repeatedly and in an amazing variety of forms. This book is aimed at exploring the Bible to identify some of the passages that testify to this claim. Further, this work hopes to invite Christians (and interested non-Christians as well) to discover a nonexcluding style of commitment to God that honors the Lord Jesus rather than continuing to crucify him by the narrowness of hate and unloving disdain for others.

I am well aware and appreciative of an explicit narrative in the Bible that focuses first on God's people, Israel, and then widens to include Christians and the church. The election of each of these peoples for specific service to God and on God's behalf in the world is clear. But there is another, implicit narrative that is the primary concern of this book; this has to do with God's ongoing relationship with others beyond Israel and the church. The service entrusted to Israel and the church assumes that all people are creatures of God and the objects of divine love. Though not the explicit story of the Bible, this implicit concern is of critical importance.

Further, though not a subject that will be developed to any great extent in this volume, my Christology, or my theological understanding about who Jesus Christ is and what he has done, is assumed as the basis for my reflections. In Jesus of Nazareth the very Logos (or Word) of God became incarnate and worked divine reconciliation. But the work of the second person of the Trinity is not identical to the work of Jesus of Nazareth. In the mystery of God other sheep have received attention. Volumes have been written in attempting to explicate how and why this has happened. Here the work of Jesus Christ provides the impetus for the effort—because God in Christ has so loved us we are impelled to love one another, even those we may first encounter as strangers or enemies. My Christology is the very source of my growing awareness of the wideness of God's love and the assurance that I can and should acknowledge others as God's children who, like me, seek to live in accordance with God's way.

In recent decades what may be called "militant extremism" in the name of religion has once again surfaced in various places around the globe. Those practicing this form of extremism deny the right of any others to exist and are willing to exercise any measure of terror (even sacrificing their own lives) toward the eradication of all they judge to be their enemies. Armed with the conviction that they alone know what God wants, they are prepared to do anything against anyone to install their vision of how things should be. Though some militant terrorists present themselves in more civilized clothing than others, the outcome is the same: God's way of love is renounced.

As yet only a few voices are being raised in challenge or protest, but it is becoming clearer by the day that another way has to be found. Few, if any, religious traditions seem to be exempt from being misused. This is a challenge that all must face. Religious exclusivism when it takes the form of militant religious extremism must be countered. In a time when the riches of religious diversity are ever more available, great opportunity exists for common action. Those who teach or practice their religious devotion in ways that encourage disdain for others by distorting and misrepresenting their own traditions and those of others need to be challenged. Hate no longer can have a legitimate place at the table of any of our religious gatherings. The resources of the major religious traditions of the world must be marshaled to develop a basis for mutual respect and just cooperation among believers and nonbelievers alike. This book is a small contribution toward this goal.

The project was made possible by the generosity of the Henry Luce III Foundation administered through the Association of Theological Schools. Additionally, Louisville Presbyterian Theological Seminary granted time and various forms of support as I worked to articulate my thoughts. A number of individuals read the manuscript in various phases of its development and offered helpful suggestions, especially James Chatham, Allan Dittmer, Susan Garrett, David Hester, and Patricia Tull. Also among these friendly critics were the members of the March-Hester adult church school class of Highland Presbyterian Church in Louisville, Kentucky, who read and reacted to the topics addressed over the course of several months. To all who aided in the completion of this project I offer genuine thanks. Finally, a word of appreciation is due the people of Westminster John Knox Press for the willingness to publish this work and for providing all of the technical assistance required to bring this book to the public. Especially I express my thanks to David Dobson, who guided the project to its completion.

It is my sincere hope that this book may be a useful resource for the serious reconsideration of Christian tradition that will enable us to join with others in addressing the numerous problems that confront us at the beginning of the twenty-first century. Solutions that are just and that sustain the dignity of all should be our goal. In the development of these we may testify to the wonder of God's gracious love, a wide, wide love, that reaches out to all.

1

Finding the Way
The Path to Follow

Chapter One

Is Religion Really a Source of Both Blessing and Curse?

*H*ad anyone been able to record the last words of the skyjackers of United Flight 175 and American Flight 11 as they crashed into the World Trade Center in New York City that fateful morning in September 2001, they might well have heard an exultant cry in Arabic: *Allahu Akbar!* "God is great!" Religion was once again claimed in the justification of a terrible act of human inhumanity—murder in the name of God!

What we have learned after that horrible morning is that the men, at least the leaders, who so carefully planned and executed the assault were militant Muslims who believed that they were carrying out an act of religious devotion. Because of their beliefs they were willing, even eager, to die for the sake of bringing devastation and death to the enemy. That the approximately three thousand people who died on September 11, 2001, were mostly innocent civilians of some ninety nations from around the world who just happened to be at the Trade Center was of little consequence. Religious fervor climaxed in catastrophic mayhem. Religion often seems more a source of curse than of blessing.

Such religious fervor is one form of what might be called "militant extremism." Extremists may be fed by political ideology just as surely, but the version that has center stage at the moment claims a religious base as its motivation. Its power rests in the assertion that its followers possess the proper, the true, understanding of the particular tradition being advocated. Many people seem to think that a kind of fanaticism is required if one desires to be a faithful adherent

3

of a religion. Rabbi David Hartman of the Shalom Hartman Institute in Jerusalem, however, has a different opinion. His organization has, with modest success, worked for several decades to bring Jews and Muslims together in search of mutual understanding and tolerance. In a conversation with columnist Thomas Friedman on the topic of such fanaticism, Rabbi Hartman asked a profound question: "Is single-minded fanaticism a necessity for passion and religious survival, or can we have a multilingual view of God—a notion that God is not exhausted by just one religious path?" (Friedman 2002, 113). It would be nice if we could answer the first question in the negative and the second in the positive, but a lot of evidence points in the opposite direction. The purpose of this book is, in part, to explore Hartman's question.

To be sure, there are and always have been a certain number of deranged people who act because of misguided beliefs. Serial killers sometime explain their acts as a response to voices they hear within, the voice of God, some indeed claim. Those who counsel the troubled often must deal with twisted understandings of the Bible and of God that warp the very capacity of the afflicted to live with others or with themselves. Family abuse has all too often been "justified" by quoting verses from the Bible. In circumstances such as these religion clearly plays a negative role. Yes, to be sure, it is religion misused by sick individuals. Nonetheless, religion is certainly part of the problem.

There is, however, a far more serious difficulty relating to the influence religious conviction exerts on all too many. Some doctrines as well as attitudes that shape large numbers of believers go well beyond the idiosyncratic behavior of some demented individuals. Some have interpreted the actions of the suicide murders of 9/11 as the acts of an atypical few. But the evidence seems to suggest that there is a much more fundamental problem in the way large numbers of Muslims are being taught the Koran and being shaped within the crucible of Islam. Extremism, or whatever one may call the virulent militancy espoused by far too many imams and mullahs in Saudi Arabia, Indonesia, Pakistan, and Germany, for instance, is twisting religious conviction into fervor for the rejection and destruction of all things Western, including especially Judaism and Christianity. This kind of religious xenophobia becomes a very negative factor in any effort to have a world where people of different faiths can live together with mutual tolerance.

But lest it seem that Muslims alone are guilty of such a misuse of religion, let's turn our attention to Christians. Militancy and violence among the faithful are hardly restricted to the adherents of only one religion. Christians too have encouraged, and at times actively supported, terrible things in the name of faithfulness to God. Three examples may suffice to make the point.

Between the years 1099 and 1291 CE, Christian rulers in Europe, actively aided by priests and other religious authorities, launched at least seven armed excursions into Palestine. These so-called Crusades were intended to free the Holy Land in general, but more particularly the holy places, from the hands of "infidels," mainly Muslims. That Muslims had built a mosque on the very site of the Holy Sepulcher was scandalous and unacceptable in the eyes of the Christian authorities living far away in Europe. Something had to be done to correct this terrible situation. Little was said about the terrible economic situation that ravaged Europe at the time or other social issues that brought fear to the hearts of the ruling class and necessitated some kind of dramatic action. No, attention was turned away and focused on the terrible plight of the Holy Land. Religious fervor was used with vigor to enlist and then sustain the crusaders on their long journey with the many great hardships they encountered. After all, these pilgrims were on a divine mission: the eradication of all nonbelievers!

In keeping with such an understanding of Christian "vocation," no quarter was shown. Old and young, armed and unarmed, male and female, Muslim and Jew, and just about any other category of human being who happened to get in the way of the crusading pilgrims was slaughtered. The Crusades were like 9/11, different in that each crusade took years to complete and involved thousands, rather than dozens, of perpetrators, but similar in that religion was the expressed motivation that justified the massacre of thousands upon thousands of people. The hymn "Onward, Christian Soldiers" (originally titled "Hymn for Procession with Cross and Banners"), though not written until 1864 CE and originally intended as a marching song for children at the festival of Whitmonday, expresses some of the triumphalism so characteristic of crusader mythology: "Onward, Christian soldiers, marching as to war, with the cross of Jesus going on before . . . ."

It should be noted that the Crusades failed in the long run. Muslim control of Palestine, except for short periods during the two centuries in question, continued. The effort to "free" the Holy Land was not successful. Generally speaking, for those who survived and remained in Palestine, that was okay, because Muslim rule was far more tolerant of other religions than that of the Christians who had sought to displace them.

The primary legacy of this expression of Christian devotion continues to be a deep distrust and disgust of the so-called Christian love extended to the Muslims of the time. Those victimized by the crusaders' form of Christian devotion certainly experienced religion, at least Christianity, as a curse rather than a blessing. "Crusade" for some Christians may be a term that evokes images of honorable knights and self-denying peasants (even children) going forth, under the banner of the cross, to fight any and all of God's enemies. But for Muslims (and for Jews as well) "crusade" is a word that symbolizes all that is twisted and ugly in human zeal to "please" God.

If the Crusades seem too distant in time to be relevant to Christian behavior in modern times—after all that was the Middle Ages—let's consider the twentieth century. Atrocity baptized in the name of religion has deeply scarred the past century, and Christians have been deeply implicated. Numerous examples demonstrate the point. Let's begin with the most obvious, the Holocaust, or Shoah, as Jews name it.

The mass murder in Europe by the Nazis of some six million men, women, and children, the vast majority of whom were Jews, during the Second World War is well documented. The Jews were singled out for one reason alone, their religion. Most Christians did not actively participate in the Nazi extermination project, but most did not resist either. German Christians, Catholic and Protestant, had developed a culture of anti-Judaism that was taught in church schools and reinforced in the regular liturgy week in and week out. Martin Luther, the German priest whose protests had begun what came to be known as the Protestant Reformation, had written scurrilous attacks on Jews back in the sixteenth century because they would not join Luther's movement. These teachings were indirectly incorporated into the life of the church. When the Nazis came to power, Luther's writings were republished and served well the Nazi propaganda program. Christian prejudice, while not virulent enough to cause most Christians to enlist in Hitler's genocidal plan, was deeply enough ingrained to reinforce widespread apathy and denial among the largely Christian population.

Further, Christian complicity was in no way restricted to Europe. Highly situated officials in the government of the United States, even the president, turned a deaf ear to repeated efforts to allow European Jews to escape the widening threat of death. Jews were turned away from entry into the United States. The military was denied permission to bomb railroad tracks used by the trains that transported Jews to the death camps. The goal of halting the slaughter of Jews in the well-known and identified camps was not considered important enough to justify the aerial intervention called for. To be sure, such a disruption in the trains would not have halted the atrocities, but toward the end of the war particularly, the Nazi plan could have been dramatically slowed. Potentially thousands of Jews might have survived. But unacknowledged religious prejudice, indeed Christian disdain for Jews, short-circuited what basic humanitarian impulse dictated.

Another dramatic example particularly rooted in the United States displays religion more as a curse than a blessing. In 1915 at Stone Mountain, Georgia, Alabama native William J. Simmons, a practicing physician and a minister of the Methodist Episcopal Church, inaugurated the "second" Ku Klux Klan. The first Klan had begun in 1866 in Pulaski, Tennessee, as a direct white supremacist response to Reconstruction in the South following the Civil War. It had waned in influence toward the end of the nineteenth century. Simmons's Klan made a major appeal to white Protestants by stressing anti-Catholic and anti-Semitic (i.e., anti-Jewish) convictions along with "nativism" (i.e., antiforeigners) and white supremacy.

After the First World War the KKK movement became national and placed a number of its sympathizers in Congress before it began its decline late in the 1920s. First introduced by Simmons, the burning cross was claimed as a symbol of Jesus Christ as the light of the world. After the Second World War there was a limited renewal of interest in the Klan, but it never regained the membership or influence it experienced in the 1920s.

Nonetheless, during the civil rights struggle of the 1950s and 1960s (and continuing to the present), the Klan, though much reduced in numbers and power, brought terror and death to many, all in the name of "true Christianity." As recently as December 2002, cross burning as an act of intimidation, was scrutinized by members of the United States Supreme Court. At issue was a Virginia law prohibiting the burning of crosses. As reported by the redding.com/newsarchive, Justice Clarence Thomas, usually rather quiet in the public proceedings of the Court, vigorously joined the debate, passionately described the burning of crosses as a dynamic symbol of hatred and oppression representing "one hundred years of lynching." The Klan's voice may have weakened, but it is by no means silent.

Unfortunately, an attitude all too similar has been in evidence in the fear and suspicion of Muslims that has abounded in the United States and elsewhere in the wake of the events of September 11, 2001. American Muslims have been subjected to a wide variety of intimidations, including death threats, arson, and other destructive acts at places of worship. There have been a number of false arrests and illegal detentions, sometimes by misguided individuals but at other times by representatives of government agencies from the local as well as the national level. Sometimes the perpetrators of these acts justify them in the name of religion. More often, such acts are rationalized as a necessary response to a false religion, in this case Islam. But to whatever degree religion plays a part, the intent and outcome have all too often been negative rather than positive.

Yes, religion—private and public—has often been used as justification for people to commit acts of violence and hate. Yes, religion—private and public—has often blinded people from recognizing injustice and has numbed people into accepting oppression while waiting for some form of heavenly relief. Yes, religion—private and public—has often been used to thwart, rather than assist, efforts to establish understanding and tolerance. Many people have been so disgusted by virulent forms of religious zeal that they have turned completely away from traditional religion, considering it more a curse than a blessing.

Nevertheless, most people do have a spiritual intelligence, a religious tendency, a desire to practice some form of religion. And many millions of people do find their lives shaped in a helpful and positive way by their religious convictions. Many African Americans have been able to endure and alter oppressive systems just because of their Christian faith. Many Jews and Christians, because of their religious convictions, were willing to take life-threatening risks to resist the Nazi fanatics. Muslims and Jews have remained true to their strongest convictions despite religious persecution by those who considered them unworthy and branded them infidels. When religious devotion survives, even flourishes, in hostile environments, it becomes worthy of careful consideration. Without denying religion's too frequent negative role, we should give attention to the positive contribution of religious faith as well. Religion may be seen as a source of blessing for many across the course of time.

Indeed, that is the case, at least from the perspective of innumerable adherents of the many religions of the world. Christians, for instance, as part of their response to the Divine, have established countless numbers of hospitals, clinics, and health programs around the world. Immunization programs and AIDS information and treatment centers have been instituted. For the sake of their work Christian doctors and teachers have lived in difficult situations amid grinding poverty, and some have been martyred. Water purification programs have been initiated. Efforts have been made to develop and teach sustainable agricultural practices. The poor have been helped to establish a wide variety of agricultural and small-business cooperatives so that they could bring their goods to market.

For Christians, evangelism has certainly been part of the larger aim. But the numerous humanitarian efforts should not be ignored or discredited as only self-serving. Often these efforts were not based on any requirement that the recipients become part of the Christian movement. In a number of Middle Eastern Muslim nations, for instance, Presbyterians have worked diligently and effectively for over a century to bring medical assistance and education to the people, all the while honoring the prohibitions imposed upon them against seeking actively to convert to Christianity the Muslims with whom they were working and serving. Other Christian denominations have a similar record in various parts of the world.

Such humanitarian efforts are evident in Muslim, Jewish, and Hindu communities—indeed, among almost all religious communities—as well. The basic needs of people are recognized and, out of religious motivation, caring people attempt to do something to make things better. Social services of all sorts are provided to persons in need who belong to the particular religious community in question, but often the services are extended to outsiders as well. To be sure, there are never sufficient resources to eradicate human suffering and need. Still, assistance is offered and some relief is given. In such instances, religion has clearly produced more blessing than curse.

Further, a host of individuals can be cited whose work serves as an example of the positive contribution religion has made to the human community. Each generation produces some outstanding leaders. From recent history there are people like Mahatma Gandhi, the great Indian Hindu, who led his people in a nonviolent revolution against British rule and for their civil liberties and political independence. Dorothy Day, a dedicated Roman Catholic, at great personal cost dedicated herself to struggle for the rights of women and for peace. Dietrich Bonhoeffer, a German Lutheran pastor, was executed by the Nazis because he took part in a plot to assassinate Adolf Hitler. Martin Luther King Jr., an African American Baptist pastor, suffered much as he led the fight against racial prejudice and injustice and for the guarantee of civil liberties, and was eventually killed because of his work. Elie Wiesel is a Jewish survivor of the Holocaust whose personal struggle to come to grips with the horrible experiences of the death camp has offered needed criticism of religious and political apathy and complicity while providing an inspiration in overcoming extraordinary suffering and justified uncertainty with respect to God. Muhammad Ali, an American Muslim and world-famous athlete, has worked tirelessly around the world as an advocate for peace and justice.

Of course there have been many others whose religious convictions led them to life-changing commitments. Mother Teresa, a Roman Catholic nun, spent her life working with the poor in India, a ministry that unexpectedly provided a wider platform for advocacy on behalf of the impoverished. Rosa Parks—an African American woman, a civil rights worker with the NAACP, and a deeply religious woman who later became a deaconess in the St. Matthews AME congregation in Detroit—on December 1, 1955, in Montgomery, Alabama, refused, mostly at the moment out of weariness rather than conviction, the demand of a white man to give up her seat on the bus. Thereby she sparked a boycott that marked the beginning of the civil rights movement in the United States and placed her in a leadership role she had not previously anticipated. Thomas Merton, a Trappist monk, wrote extensively on mysticism, peace, and interfaith dialogue and thereby influenced countless people to reflect upon the connection between faith and life. Because of his Christian faith, Jimmy Carter, after leaving the presidency of the United States, has worked zealously in and on behalf of the Habitat for Humanity program aimed at providing good housing for low-income people. Zaynab al-Ghazali, no doubt considered a "radical" by many, founded the Muslim Women's Association in Egypt, a group that has maintained an orphanage, encouraged women to study Islam, and has worked diligently to assist poor families in finding useful employment. All of these individuals, at least in part because of their religious commitments, have brought blessing to the human communities in which they have lived and worked.

The point of all this is that history offers irrefutable evidence that religion can be and has been both a curse and a blessing. Further, although it seems blatantly obvious to say it, there is a significant difference between those who take the course of what has been referred to above as "militant extremism" and those who do not. If one begins with the conviction that there is only one right way, namely "my way" or "our way," then other people become objects to be fashioned by whatever means necessary to fit the "right way." Militant extremism requires that all other views, and those who hold them, must be challenged, and then corrected (converted) or destroyed. Humanitarian service may be a useful strategy in the service of this goal, but it can never be primary. For those on the receiving end of such a program, religion is usually experienced as a curse.

In its most virulent forms militant extremism spawns terrorists committed to imposing their view of the world on all those around them no matter what the cost. There is finally no room for the "other" and no reason for tolerance or civil discourse aimed at bettering the whole human community.

Militant extremism in its most highly publicized recent form in the West is of a militant Muslim version, but there are plenty of examples of the same attitude among Christian and Jewish groups that could be cited, from the past and in the present. Openness and respect toward others is what the world needs. Intolerance, especially in the name of religion, can only bring disaster. That makes it imperative that moderate leaders and teachers of all religions address this problem and lead the devout along a different path.

The vision espoused here, and shared by many others representing a variety of religious traditions in our world, requires the recognition of the wideness of divine love. God has been in relationship with human beings as long as they have existed, in a multitude of contexts and in a variety of ways. The defeat of militant extremism entails, in part, recognizing this fact and embracing the divine love offered so freely to the world. Part of the evidence for this understanding is the very existence of the religions of the world and the motivation religious conviction has often provided for bringing blessing to the world. Religious devotion does not have to become militant extremism. Indeed, religious devotion, rightly informed by the positive richness of religious tradition, can and should be a most healthy antidote against the militant hate that still infects the world.

Chapter Two

Is Religious Diversity a Divine Blunder?

*I*t is currently estimated that there are more than fifteen hundred active religions in the world. To be sure, some can claim only a very small number of adherents and some are clearly subsets of larger entities. In a world with an estimated population of some six and a quarter billion and still counting, over five billion are claimed as members of one religion or another. This multiplicity of religions is called "religious pluralism" or "religious diversity." To acknowledge this great diversity of religions, each believed to be valid by its adherents, is not to endorse each and every one, but it is to recognize current realities. Religions abound!

What are we to make of this? In antiquity it was assumed that everyone was religious. There were certainly those who did not attend to religious duty to the extent that their neighbors thought prudent. Some did not sacrifice with sufficient devotion or zeal. Some did not maintain the traditions sufficiently. Some, like the Greek poet Euripides (480–406 BCE) and the Roman Stoic philosopher Persius (34–62 CE), offered criticism (sometimes quite satirical) of religious practice that seemed to have become merely superstition and magic. Later, at the beginning of the Common Era, Jews and Christians were often charged as "atheists" because neither group would offer sacrifices to idols, and particularly not to the emperor. Still, the general assumption was held that there were deities who required or deserved proper service or worship to ensure individual and communal well-being. Different peoples honored different gods and goddesses, but religion was part of life.

Across the centuries, particularly in the West (Europe and North America mainly), the authenticity of religion has come under fire. There have been those who, in the course of presenting the intellectual history of the West, have described religious conviction as a "childish" or "primitive" phase in the development of civilization. According to these voices, modern people could and should put aside belief in supernatural powers and assume responsibility for the good and the bad that people encounter in the course of life. The role of reason and the triumph of science have successfully challenged the dominance once exercised by religion. There is simply no need for religion, these critics say. Indeed, much of what is wrong with the world could be ascribed to overly zealous, uncritically trusting adherents of religion. In the West, Christianity is the religion being most frequently challenged.

In the last decade of the twentieth century, however, new evidence of a religious resurgence arose. In the West, large numbers of people from a great variety of backgrounds have shown amazing interest in books and groups that espouse spirituality. Many of these people do not belong to any established religion, but they do believe in a Reality that is beyond them. They believe that one can tap in to that Other through various spiritual practices such as prayer, meditation, yoga, and fasting. Beyond the bounds of organized religion, spirituality has become a common denominator for a vastly diverse throng of people eclectically drawing from all manner of material in a quest to experience inner peace and to fashion some form of unifying interpretation of life. To be sure, within recognized religions there is renewed interest in spirituality as well.

In light of all this, the question again arises: What are we to make of all this religion? Christian theology across the centuries has tended either to ignore the reality of the diverse and numerous religions in the world or to condemn all other religions as irreligion, as paganism, as falsehood. Moreover, Christians in the West, until very recently, have lived for the most part in situations where people of other religions (Judaism being the exception) rarely existed. Thus, for many, the reality of other religions was largely unrecognized and certainly unappreciated. When acknowledged at all, other religions were viewed mostly as evidence for the need to send out messengers for the purpose of converting these "nonbelievers," these non-Christians, to the true religion.

Now, however, at least in many metropolitan areas in the United States and Canada, Muslims, Sikhs, Buddhists, Zoroastrians, Shintoists, Confucianists, and members of other faiths as well, live in the neighborhood and are met in the workplace by the Christians and Jews who have long lived side by side. The reality of other, nonbiblical religions is no longer hypothetical or only an issue if one ventures "over there." Other religions are here and adherents of these religions have names and faces. "Their" children go to school with "ours." In the United States and Canada they are full citizens with all the same privileges and obligations. Are their religious beliefs all wrong? If so, is their "error" dangerous? Do they have to be Christian to be acknowledged as legitimately religious and in authentic relationship with the Divine? How do their religious convictions challenge or perhaps enrich ours?

For many centuries, as noted in the preceding chapter, the vast majority of Christians assumed that Christianity was the only valid religion. All other religions were pagan and thus, at best, to be ignored or, at worst, to be destroyed. Christian faith, it was believed, required the rejection of all other traditions. There was no other way into a meaningful relationship with God except through faith in Jesus. Christians alone had a saving relationship with God, and that was all there was to it. All other religions were false, even harmful in many instances.

This attitude had a number of consequences in the course of history. The Crusades in the eleventh to thirteenth centuries of Common Era were an expression of this narrow religious worldview. Christians slaughtered countless Muslims and Jews—in fact, anyone who got in their way—in an effort to reclaim the Holy Land of Palestine as the exclusive site for Christian devotion and pilgrimage. The conquest of the New World in the fifteenth to seventeenth centuries with the killing of vast numbers of indigenous peoples was rationalized, in part, as necessary to "save" these folk from their pagan ways and make them Christian, either peaceably or by force as necessary.

In the nineteenth century a great project was undertaken to evangelize the world, to convert the "heathen" in all quarters of the earth to Christianity. This was done out of the sincere conviction that all the non-Christians of the world faced the terrible, but inevitable, prospect of eternal punishment unless they could be brought to faith in Christ. Believing that Christ is the only way to a saving relationship with God was the unchallenged motivator for interaction with people of non-Christian conviction. The non-Christians needed something that Christians alone had, namely the love of God. To remedy this situation, a vigorous effort to convert all the peoples of the world was launched. There was genuine love for the "heathen," a deep desire that all might experience the love of God that Christians realized in their relationship with Jesus Christ. But all too often there was also great misunderstanding of and disdain for the religious traditions of those "others" encountered on the mission field.

There were notable successes in the mission effort. Christianity took hold on the Korean peninsula, for instance, and in many parts of sub-Saharan Africa. Indigenous churches developed, some of which now surpass in membership the American and European bodies that first evangelized them. The Wycliffe Bible Translators report that at the end of 2002 all or parts of the Bible have been translated into 2,233 of the estimated 6,500 languages of the world. There was often no written form of the spoken language, and thus linguists first had to create a written version so that the translation work could be done. Hospitals and schools were built. Human need was addressed, all in the belief that God commanded and expected the extension of Christianity throughout the whole wide world.

But there was a downside that is only now becoming alarmingly clear. First, the mission enterprise was inextricably bound with colonialism. Parallel to the spread of Christian missionaries, there was also an extensive process of political and economic expansion by European nations, and later by the United States. This imperialism shaped the way people were governed and the way business was done. The underlying assumption was that the West truly represented the highest form of civilization that had yet evolved. In every respect—including religion—the ways of the West were simply superior to those of the rest of the world. Westerners believed that the only proper response on the part of the "others" should be gratitude and relief that the West had come to their rescue.

Of course, we now know that those who were being "saved" did not always appreciate the efforts of the "saviors." The Christian message was far too closely packaged in a social/economic/political/cultural wrap that was distinctly and unnecessarily European and North American. The centuries-old practice of polygamy in Africa, for instance, was attacked as totally incompatible with Christian values, even though the practice is clearly documented in the Old Testament, or "First Testament" as some Christians prefer to call it, or the Bible as Jews call it. There was little or no effort made to understand the social and economic consequences of the demand the missionaries made for the denunciation of polygamy.

At the same time, the rejection of slavery as un-Christian was not so universally demanded, at least not in the early years of the missionary effort. Indeed, unlike polygamy, slavery was often defended on the basis of the Bible. The economic effects of the elimination of slavery were unacceptable "back home." Further, especially among those who were "saved," it did not go unnoticed that the "saviors" had, generally speaking, a much more comfortable (even lavish at times) lifestyle in their cultural oases of privilege.

What seems so clear in hindsight is that there was great confusion as to what was European and American culture and what was actually Christian. Christianity has existed for many centuries in many different places. Christians always necessarily reflect the culture in which they live. That is unavoidable and is not wrong. What was wrong, however, with the Christian expansion of the nineteenth and twentieth centuries was the uncritical wedding of Western culture with the Christian message. Christian outreach came to be viewed by many as simply a disguise for economic and cultural imperialism on the part of the great colonial powers of the era, particularly Great Britain, Germany, France, Spain, Portugal, and the Netherlands. To some degree before but especially since the end of the Second World War, the United States has, in the eyes of many, become the leader of Western imperialism and exploitation. Globalization is the new mantra, but the disdain for others and the assumed superiority of American culture over all other cultures are not new in the way the West continues to relate to the rest of the world.

A more positive appreciation of other religious traditions is needed today and requires a different approach. Instead of assuming that since Christianity is true all other beliefs must be false, let's begin at another place. Let's reflect on the wonder of creation. One of the most notable aspects of the world in which we live is the great diversity we find, among the living and the nonliving. Within any category there are uncountable sets and subsets. How many varieties of butterflies are there to delight the eye? How many birds are there to make a mess on the town square and eat the fig trees bare? Or how many types of trees are spread around the world? There are over forty just in my neighborhood. And how about rocks and gems? As a child I started collecting rocks. I thought I had done a good job of gathering all the kinds of stones there were. Then I was given a box that held thirty-six examples of geologic wonders that I had never even seen or imagined, and this was just a starter set for the would-be geologist.

Then, of course, there is the human family. Try sitting in the mall and counting the categories of people who happen by. "Different" is the operative word. While ethnicity and gender might offer two immediate measures, neither is finally sufficient. Each individual is unique. Differences are seemingly infinite. Indeed, apart from a rare set of twins or triplets, everyone looks different. Sure, there are clothing designs and hairstyles that make us look similar, but we recognize our friends easily. Thousands, millions, billions of human beings, all similar but distinct from one another, each with inherent value and potential.

The diversity within our world is something most of us take for granted. There are in the neighborhood of fifty million species of plants and animal life currently to be found, and it is estimated that perhaps as many as fifty billion have existed at one time or another across the long lifespan of our world. Difference is simply obvious: different flowers, different animals, different languages, different people. Wouldn't one kind of butterfly or bird have been sufficient? Apparently not, because variety seems to be the way things are supposed to be.

So why should there not be different religions? Why should we be surprised or troubled by the reality of different ways to express spirituality? Since diversity seems to be the norm in creation, by analogy a pluralism of religious responses among the people of the world is reasonable to expect. Indeed, a rich diversity of cultures and religions is what we encounter in the world. Just as within the worlds of plants and insects and fish and cattle and on and on, so within the human world there have been and continue to be numerous expressions of religious interest and concern.

How are we to react to such a world, a world with great diversity and numerous religious traditions? What sense can we make of our reality? No one seems disturbed by the great variety of snakes or beans or trees or precious and semiprecious stones. It does not seem important or truthful to deny the reality or value of terriers in defense of a preference for spaniels. Diversity does not have to be seen as a liability or as the result of a confused Creator who used multiplicity as a way to disguise an inability to settle on one breed over another. Certainly religious expression is at least as important before God as the variety of canine breeds.

The trouble comes from within the human family when one group assumes that it alone has the truth and then claims the right to assert itself over another. As we have seen, such a response of Christians to others has had terrible consequences. Is there another way? Can Christians acknowledge the authenticity of other faiths without denying their own convictions? This is a question that is imperative to explore.

In the Bible God is said to have looked upon the whole of creation and declared it "very good" (Genesis 1:31). Of course, according to the biblical account, the vast diversities within the human family had not yet materialized, but gender differentiation had occurred and all the other variations of creation are alluded to. The evidence from the created order seems to be that variation, differences, should be not only expected but also celebrated. If the Creator deemed creation to be very good with all the diversity found therein, shouldn't we also come to the same conclusion?

But even among Christians there are profound differences of understanding on this point. According to some Christians, while the world as initially created was indeed good, that is not the world we now live in. Creation suffered a catastrophic "fall" as a result of human sin. All the good that God created was corrupted by sin and thus is no longer good. The bad results of sin are basically manifest in the breakdown of the social order and by the inhumanities that mark too much of the interaction between individuals and communities. Furthermore, the physical order is negatively affected as well by this fall and yearns with humanity for redemption, to be made whole and good once more, to be restored to a harmonious relationship with God. The religions of the world—some Christians would include Christianity as well—attest to human longing for the Divine, but because of sin such longings are doomed to failure.

The response of these Christians to the world as they understand it is to announce the good news of Jesus Christ with the hope that sinners will be converted and the human institutions corrupted by sin will be transformed. Only God can finally accomplish such a task, but the good news is that God in Christ is well on the way toward this end. The kingdom of God is breaking in. The days of sin and death are numbered.

This is a hopeful message, but human history offers little concrete evidence to support a view that much headway has been made toward God's purpose in the twenty centuries since the death and resurrection of Jesus of Nazareth. Many individuals have certainly come to know the saving love of God, but vast numbers of people in the world, in fact roughly two-thirds, are still following ways other than the Christian way. These people believe that their religions are both meaningful and adequate to meet their needs. Is it necessary to deny or attack the faith of others in order to maintain and defend one's own?

The Bible suggests that there is an alternative possibility. The Bible does teach that sin is a serious source of destructive behavior that disrupts human relationships within the human family and with God. But it is not necessary to conclude from this that the whole of creation is now contaminated by human sin. Creation is still good. Creation thankfully does provide a source for reflection on the purposes of God. The diversity of the created order and the diversity of human experience are important to consider. The variety seen all around us suggests that variety is part of the divine intention. Pluralism, diversity, seems more godlike than not. Christians can emphasize the common good found among all people and can share their understanding of God and their experience of God with others without denying from the outset the experience and knowledge of others.

The Bible offers accounts of many different people in many different contexts recognizing and experiencing God

This brings us back to our initial question: What shall we think about the vast array of religious belief that is evident in our world? The traditional Christian view seems to imply that all the non-Christian people of the world exist primarily to provide a mission field for dedicated evangelists. In extreme forms of this position, it is believed that most of the people in the world have been damned by God before they are even born. Thus there is no need to fret that the vast majority of human beings are not, nor ever will be, brought to salvation in Christ. Other religions are at best the erroneous result of misguided people searching for God, and at worst represent demonic efforts to ensnare and bring to destruction those chosen by God to become Christian and to know redemption.

Another answer to our question, however, is being voiced more and more in recent decades. Other religions, according to this alternative view, are a clear sign of God at work in the midst of the human family in many different cultures and in many different times. The non-Christian religions are also the work of God's creative power. They are not the result of a divine blunder. God is neither inept nor uncaring. God is a gracious Creator who providentially provides for all people. It is in acknowledging the diversity of God's creation just as in marveling at all the different kinds of people that Jesus loved so deeply that we will recognize the incredible goodness of God and the fullness of God's purpose.

Christians do have a special calling, but it is not to lord it over others or to deny the validity of the beliefs and experiences of others. We will turn to this important subject later. But for now it is crucial to affirm that other religions have an equally important place in God's world. Sikhs and Taoists are part of God's divine handiwork. Muslims, Jews, and Buddhists offer significant contributions to understanding the diversity of religious experience. These expressions of religion are precious to God and thus should be honored by all who call themselves religious.

Be under no illusion. This alternative view is not the position of most Christians, at least not at present. But it is a legitimate interpretation based on a significant number of biblical passages. These passages have often been ignored or interpreted from a position of assumed superiority to substantiate the belief that other religions are inferior at best and totally wrong at worst. Though the exclusive superiority of Christianity has often been championed with great vigor (and sometime even vehemence), the Bible suggests a much more tempered understanding. Our next task, then, is to turn to the Bible to see just what is said and what is not said. There will be no effort to claim that the whole Bible supports the position we are considering. Nonetheless, a biblical base can be demonstrated in support of this alternative position. There is important witness to the claim that the religious convictions of non-Christians are not at all the result of a divine mistake or divine inadequacy.

But before we turn to the Bible, we have one more question to consider. Must only one religion be true?

Chapter Three

Must Only One Religion Be True?

Larry King Live and *Donahue* may not be the best places to go for in-depth information on any topic, especially religion, but each show does provide a barometer for current public opinion. A review of the programming of these shows quickly reveals that religion continues to be a draw, guaranteed to engender heated reactions, though usually not much clarity. One of the recurring subjects on these and other radio and TV talk shows centers on whether more than one religion can be true at the same time. Or, as the issue is often posed, at least in Christian circles, Do you have to be a Christian to get to heaven?

That, in fact, was the title of Phil Donahue's show on December 17, 2002. There were representatives of several identifiable Christian and Jewish groups, including conservatives and liberals, on the panel. Claims and counterclaims flew. Donahue played the role of gadfly, especially toward the conservatives. Audience participation was solicited and readily forthcoming. For some, the issue was easily settled by quoting a few verses from the New Testament, primarily the Gospel of John. According to this group of Christians, there is no question. Those who do not believe in Jesus simply have no hope of heaven. For other Christian and Jewish participants, however, such an approach was quite unacceptable, simplistic at best and arrogant at worst, epitomizing the ignorance and disregard Christians often have for the religious experience of others. At the very least, some of these moderates contend that Christians should exercise greater humility in considering this issue. After all, God alone is in a position to decide who is in and who is out or whether this matters at all.

No consensus emerged—surprise! And it seems unlikely that many opinions were changed. But the topic is a good one that deserves continuing attention. Do you have to be a Christian to get to heaven? How one decides the matter does affect the way one views others and one's understanding of the role religion plays within the human community. Is religious extremism, or what has also been called "religious totalitarianism"—my way alone is right and all others are to be destroyed—the only way? Is God's love intended for only a fraction of the human community? Can human language exhaustively, or even adequately, articulate the fullness of God's truth? Is heaven large enough for the great diversity of human beings that populate the globe, most of whom believe that they are worshiping God truly? Or to put it more simply, must only one religion be true?

This side of heaven, there is no way to answer the last question conclusively, one way or the other. People may believe what they want, but there is simply no way to prove their beliefs to be correct. But it is important to acknowledge that there are several different approaches that true believers of various faith communities do take in response to the perplexing question. There is no one party line that all Christians adopt. Not all Muslims want to relate to those of other religions with the harsh militancy of the clerics of the Taliban, for instance. Hindus by and large have demonstrated a remarkable capacity for tolerance and respect of others, though they have clashed seriously with Muslims at various times, especially in the last two decades. Most Jews take a live-and-let-live approach to the matter of religious diversity. And Christians? Yes, there are some card-carrying, serious Christian believers, baptized once or perhaps twice, who acknowledge not only the reality but even the legitimacy of other religions.

Of course, one must acknowledge from the outset that, as far as the church is concerned, the historical position on the question of who can go to heaven has been that only Christians could count on making it. Indeed, the earliest form of this doctrine held that only those who *belonged to the church* could be saved, and "church" was understood in a very concrete way that for at least one thousand years meant the Roman Catholic Church. To be sure, the Greek Orthodox

Church has always maintained that it was and is the one true church and considered Rome to be in error. In either case, church membership was the deciding factor.

After the Protestant Reformation in the sixteenth century, Protestants insisted that the only qualification for salvation was faith in Jesus Christ, and this was not to be connected in any absolute way to membership in the church. Usually, of course, faith led to baptism and church membership, but faith alone was finally all that counted when passes to heaven were distributed. Some Protestant creedal statements did acknowledge that there might well be some who would be saved by God's mercy, people who in fact were never outwardly connected with the church or had never made explicit confession of faith in Jesus. But believers constituted the primary crowd who would stand before God's eternal throne forever and forever.

At present many Christians assume unquestioningly the singular validity of Christianity. The Bible, they believe, teaches that there is only one way to God, namely Jesus Christ. Thus all other ways must be false and misguided. Most Christians do not want to seem mean about the matter, however, and thus express sorrow at the fate of all the non-Christians. In recent years there has even been extended discussion and debate about whether God will save infants and children, for instance, who meet untimely deaths before coming to faith, or redeem "infidels" who live exemplary lives but die never having had the opportunity to hear the gospel of Jesus Christ. Still, there is only one right religion, Christianity, and more often than not, only a certain brand of Christianity, namely "my" denomination!

In the scholarly world of comparative religion, the position thus far described is called "exclusivist." The central tenet is that "my" religion is the only true religion. All other religions are wrong. Thus the claims of all others must be disputed. Others may be tolerated for a time, but this is only a strategy imposed by circumstance. The goal is to eliminate all other faiths by persuasion or conquest, whichever is most expedient. The world is divided into those who believe correctly and those who do not, and ultimately there is room for only the true religion to survive. Pragmatically, believers may have to live in the midst of pluralism, but there is no doubt to them that all other ways are forms of rebellion against God

Vast numbers of Christians have accepted the exclusivist position quite uncritically. The interpretations of the biblical passages quoted to prove the correctness of this approach have generally gone unchallenged. In the West, contact with persons of other faith communities has been practically nonexistent until the second half of the twentieth century. Thus there was no experiential basis from which to raise questions about the assumptions being announced as "truth." There did not seem to be any obvious negative consequences in taking an exclusivist position, hence many have accepted this stance believing it to be the necessary choice of all who desire to be faithful Christians.

The exclusivist position is certainly not restricted to Christians. Some Jews and some Muslims also hold such a view. They may not attack others, at least not in the North American context, but they see no reason to interact with others. They dismiss the religious claims of others as unimportant or as wrong.

Not infrequently, forms of nationalism also become closely identified with exclusive religious commitments, among Christians as well as others. The mantra becomes "my religion and my nation" alone have the truth and alone are right. The combination of religious and nationalistic exclusiveness all too often breeds fanaticism that has terrible consequences for all involved.

During the last half of the twentieth century, however, another position has emerged, the inclusive interpretation of religions. Persons with an inclusive perspective consider their own religion to offer the best but not the only possible understanding of the Divine. For Christians this means that God is most fully revealed in Jesus Christ. God's work is brought to its completion in Jesus Christ. The best, the most satisfying, the most secure, the most fulfilling relationship with God is to be found in faithfully following Jesus Christ. But such a commitment to Jesus does not require a denunciation of all other religious views.

For Christians who take the inclusive position, people of other religions are believed to have glimpsed the truth. They may not be experiencing the fullest possible relationship with God, but they do have an authentic relationship with the Divine. Their moral teachings are often illumining and instructive. Their visions of peace and harmony are complementary to those of Christians. Thus adherents of other religions are to be respected as people loved by God. Christians can share with and learn from people of other faiths. Amid all the differences, there are things that Christians can and should hold in common with others. The differences are not ignored, but they are not the point of emphasis. Christians who hold this position see others as on the right road, perhaps, but not as far along toward the goal of full relationship with God that Christians enjoy. Respect and the desire to share mark this stance rather than an attitude of disdain or the demand to convert.

Along with some Christians, Hindus have long adopted this basic approach to other religions. Numerous Jews and Muslims share such an understanding. Among the living religions, however, Baha'i possibly best exemplifies the institutionalizing of this position. That is, the legitimacy of all religions is one of the basic beliefs of the Baha'i. While not naming their position "inclusive," members of Baha'i have, in effect, taken this basic stance for many years. They believe their own religion is the best, but they acknowledge and respect the beliefs of others.

Baha'i is a religion that developed in the nineteenth century. Though originally related to Islam, it no longer retains any connection with that base. It is monotheistic and believes that all religions are the work of God. The equality of all human beings is a fundamental belief. Education is a high priority. Often criticized as being eclectic, Baha'i has learned from the experience of others as well as from its own. To see the good in other religions is not always easy and is frequently considered dangerous by those who exercise power in the religious arena. The inclusive position of the Baha'i, however, expresses no need to scapegoat others or to see others as a threat. The history of Baha'i demonstrates the glories and dangers of the inclusive position. The Baha'i have often been persecuted just because of their tolerance. But for others who have come to know the Baha'i, admiration abounds.

Yet a third approach that some are taking is known among scholars as the "pluralist" position. The basic assumption is that all religions are essentially equal in that each represents a legitimate human response to the Divine. Some forms of religion may be more "sophisticated" and "developed" than others, but no single religious tradition has a corner on truth. Each religion seeks to enable its adherents to experience God more fully. Each religion must be evaluated in terms of its own claims and in its own context. Every religion has produced believers who have demonstrated good and bad behaviors. Comparisons that claim one religion is better or worse than others are not appropriate. The reality is that there is an enormous plurality of religious expression with each pointing in some way or another to the Divine that defines all that exists.

While not many religious people immediately identify with the pluralist position, many do—at least in the West—adopt a way of dealing with other religions that fits the approach. Many people on the street explain other religions in relation to their own as simply different paths to the same destination. A live-and-let-live attitude toward those of different faiths is practiced. Sometimes the judgment is expressed that it is better to believe something rather than nothing or that all of us walk by our own light. Many people believe that God in some way indwells each person in the form of a divine spark, or spirit, or archetype. Each person's beliefs are assumed valid for that individual and are to be honored insofar as they do not result in the attacking or degrading of others. There is respect for the mutuality of shared commitments. In the pluralistic democracy of the United States, Americans tend to grant others the right to believe whatever they choose. Supporting this tolerance is the conviction of many that all religions are essentially equal, the differences representing taste and family tradition rather than compelling views of the truth.

Fewer people who are actively engaged in a faith community tend to adopt the pluralist position. By reason of their involvement in a particular faith they tend to assume that their religion alone is valid (exclusive) or that among all the other possibilities it is the best (inclusive). But a growing number of people who have carefully studied the religions of the world find the pluralist position the most honest in light of the evidence. As Christians they may have a personal allegiance to Jesus, but they recognize that the commitments of a Buddhist or a Muslim or a Hindu have integrity and substance. There is growing willingness to accept the validity of the faiths of others and celebrate true differences. These pluralists pose the greatest threat to the exclusivists and are thus vehemently attacked by the orthodoxy police who dominate religious programming on radio and TV. Nonetheless, this position is widely held, at least informally, and has much to commend it.

With respect to the original question, Do you have to be a Christian to get to heaven? significantly different answers are given according to one's foundational assumptions. The exclusive position is that no one of another faith will be received into heaven. If a Christian is responding, then it is only other Christians (but not necessarily all who call themselves Christian) who may be delivered. If a Shiite Muslim answered the inquiry from the exclusive stance, then only certain followers of Muhammad, not all, could hope for paradise. By its very nature, the exclusive stance assumes that far more people will not make it into heaven than will.

From the inclusive point of view, a far greater number of people may get to heaven since God alone, not doctrine or institution, will determine the issue. A Christian will believe that Christ's way is the most expeditious and reliable, but other ways do offer some light and in God's mercy that light may be sufficient. An inclusive Jew might well consider the question a quaint relic of Christian anxiety. Certainly God can and will preserve (in some fashion) the memory of each individual, and Judaism provides the best guidance toward that goal, but people of other faiths will (in fact, already do) share in the generous mercy of God.

For those coming from the pluralist point of view the question must be rephrased in order to have much relevance at all. The issue from a pluralist stance is, How do the many religions each guide believers to fellowship with the Divine? Christians will certainly not be the only ones to get to heaven, and they should not wish to be. Human experience of God is fantastically varied, presenting a rich tapestry on which to place all human hopes and expectations. For some Buddhists "heaven" may be attaining the capacity to move beyond enslaving desires to live in harmony with the Divine. For Jews who are not seeking heaven, the fulfillment of religious devotion comes from studying God's ways and working for a society that more fully reflects those ways. The point is that, as pluralists view the question, the real issue is what is intended in the asking of it. Some Christians assume that getting to heaven is the aim of all religions.

Pluralists recognize that there may be other aims, other intentions, that stand at the heart of other religions, and insist that these intentions be honored in their own right.

As noted at the outset, no one answer can be conclusively demonstrated to be true. The differing views held by various religions are considered by their adherents to be valid. It is clear that believers of various religions do consider their religion to provide some measure of light, but what is done with that conviction depends greatly on whether one is exclusive, inclusive, or pluralistic in one's overall approach to religion. If the poison of militant extremism that is nourished by religious conviction is to be neutralized, however, the inclusive and pluralistic positions seem to offer the most effective antidote available.

Among the many religions and many religious people in the world, no single faith community has a uniformly good or bad record in human affairs. Each religion offers a mixed bag when measured in terms of how well people are enabled to live more justly, humanely, and trustingly before God. There are crazies in every group. Some religious traditions seem more sensitive to ethical concerns and more able to provide assurance to believers. But at the level of objective evaluation, and apart from the insistence of the advocates, there is no conclusive evidence to suggest that there is only one true religion.

For believers who belong to the three religions that claim Abraham and Sarah and Hagar as forebears, the tradition of each has long maintained the singular validity of each particular form, whether Judaism, Christianity, or Islam. Of course, rationally speaking, all cannot be the true religion. Each may witness to the truth, but all three cannot at the same time represent the only way that God and humanity can be related. If each of these religions had one by one replaced the preceding version of the Abrahamic tradition, thereby invalidating its predecessor, then there would not be a difficulty. (And exclusivists in each tradition claim that that is exactly the case.) But that is not what has happened historically or theologically. Judaism, Christianity, and Islam continue as vital religions with numerous adherents, each meeting the needs and desires of those who participate in those particular faith communities. A Christian may deem Judaism or Islam as inadequate, but a Jew or Muslim will no doubt make the same judgment about Christianity. This whole question becomes all the more opaque when the wider universe of religions is introduced.

So what can be done to unsnarl this knot? Empirical evidence presents a plethora of religious claims. The personal experience of any one of us, at least if it is wide enough, attests to numerous people of other faiths who are at least as good as we are and who credit God with being the source of their convictions and the strength of their lives. Rationally speaking, then, it is just as easy to say that no religion is true as it is that only one religion is true. So why have so many claimed so loudly for so long to represent the only way to God? Almost always, the answer to that question is to be found in a lack of genuine, firsthand knowledge of the religious beliefs of others and in the manner in which the religious texts of their own community are interpreted. Little can be done to fill gaps in personal experience, but texts can be carefully considered and interpretations reviewed. Just because "we have always understood it that way" does not guarantee that a passage cannot and should not be read differently in a new time and place.

The assumption that there must be only one religion—that only Christians, or only Jews, or only you-fill-in-the-blank can get to heaven—should not be the starting point for interpretation. Because some people still believe the world is flat, they claim that the photographs of Earth taken from space cannot possibly be authentic or accurate. To begin with the belief that "my religion alone can be true" will surely color the reading of the Bible or whatever particular holy writing happens to be involved.

The reading and interpreting of holy texts is not as easy as it might first appear. Most scripture was first written by people who lived many hundreds of years ago, often in social settings and historical circumstances almost totally unknown to most modern readers. The Bible, for instance, was written between two and three thousand years ago in three different languages, Hebrew, Aramaic, and Greek. The oldest complete manuscripts we now have were written in the late fourth and early fifth centuries CE, or, in other words, at least three hundred years after the time of Jesus. There is no existing original of any of the biblical books.

The worldview of the writers was distinctly different from that of contemporary readers, especially in the West. Most Christians believe that God inspired the writers of the Bible, but they still wrote in the language of their day and in the style and rhetoric of their time. When they used a term like "world," for instance, they did so with no knowledge at all of the Western Hemisphere or even of much of the Eastern Hemisphere. When they described their "world," they assumed it was flat and had four corners. This does not disqualify their message, not at all, but it does mean that care must be taken in determining exactly what the message is. We should not understand their world as the equivalent of ours. What is required, therefore, is careful attention to the historical context, the social context, and the literary context of each passage. Professional retailers often insist that the secret to business success is "location, location, location!" For responsible interpretation of ancient writings the key is context, context, context!

In light of some of the continuing tragedies perpetrated in the name of religion, a new look at the convictions on which such actions are based is in order. For most Christians, the place to begin is with the Bible, and so we will now turn to the task of rereading the Scriptures in order to shed some light on the subject. What does the Bible really say with regard to our question? The claims have long been heard, but what about the texts themselves that are used to buttress the assumption that only Christians will get to heaven?

The exploration will take us to two primary narratives in Genesis, those presenting Noah and Abraham, two figures that represent humankind as a whole well before they are connected to Jewish, Christian, and Muslim tradition. Then there will follow reflections on passages from the Prophets, the wisdom literature, and finally the New Testament, particularly the Gospels of Luke and John. The full biblical tradition cannot be examined, but a significant set of passages clearly suggests the need to consider the biblical message anew, reading from the awareness of the wideness rather than the narrowness of God's gracious, creative, passionate love.

The Bible itself may well surprise and offer a better way than has all too often been claimed as the "biblical way." Context, context, context—that is the key!

2

Finding the Truth
The Path Less Noticed

Chapter Four

After the Cruise: God's New Beginning

*T*he first book of the Bible, Genesis, is about origins: who we are as humans, where we came from, what is our purpose. The first chapters tell of a common beginning symbolized in the figures of Adam and Eve and then a decline of the human family into sinful chaos punctuated by Cain's murder of his brother Abel. Then a new episode is introduced when God decides for both a destroying judgment and a renewing deliverance made particular through a man named Noah.

Noah is famous for a cruise he and his family took at the instruction of God. Perhaps it was not a cruise in the contemporary sense of the word, but it was a long voyage in a boat. The trip was made necessary because God brought a great flood upon the earth to destroy all sinners in order to start afresh with the human creatures fashioned in the divine image. The details of this episode are recounted in the first book of the Bible, Genesis 6–9.

Let's consider some of the particulars of this biblical story. Noah was five hundred years plus when he was told to build an ark or boat. (This ark is not to be confused with the boxlike container, the ark of the covenant, housed in Jerusalem until the Temple was destroyed in 587 BCE. That ark has, in modern times, become an object of mystic speculation and cinematic adventure in the film *Raiders of the Lost Ark.*) The dimensions of the boat are given as 300 by 50 by 30 cubits. As best we know, a cubit was between 17 and 20 inches in length. This means that Noah's vessel would have been roughly 500 feet in length, 84 feet wide, and 50 feet tall. It had three levels, or decks, for Noah's family and all the cargo he had to bring on board. It was basically a barge like those that have, from time immemorial, traversed the great rivers of the world. Some ancient wood-hull ships documented in Egyptian, Greek, and Roman records were as much as 200 feet long and 25 to 30 feet wide. The *Santa Maria* that Christopher Columbus sailed across the Atlantic is estimated to have been roughly 60 by 20 by 10 feet. In comparison, Noah's boat was big! Yes, it was smaller than the *Titanic* (883 by 92 by 60 feet), though not by much, but still, by any measure, it was large. Not bad for a hand-built barge!

According to the story, Noah, his wife, and his three sons with their wives entered the ark as the rain began and did not leave the ark for a year and ten days. Noah took on board a male and female (or perhaps seven pairs of the clean animals depending, on certain verses) of every living creature in order that they might survive the disaster. Of course, though this is not directly mentioned, food provisions for a year for all the human and nonhuman voyagers had to be taken on board as well. The logistics of it all are staggering.

The flood began with rain, but the tremendous amount of water needed to cover the highest mountain with at least 25 feet of water, as the story recounts, mostly came from the cosmic waters that were believed to encircle the world. As the story puts it, the "windows of the heavens" were opened and the "fountains of the great deep" gushed forth and the whole earth was deluged with water. The primordial waters mentioned in the opening verses of Genesis 1 flooded the world, destroying every living creature except for those preserved on Noah's ark (Genesis 7:11–12, 18–22).

When the waters finally subsided months later, the ark rested on an unspecified summit among the "mountains of Ararat," identified in modern times as the Urartian mountain range located in the extreme eastern section of modern Turkey. Because it is the highest and most spectacular mountain in the range, a summit named anachronistically "Mount Ararat," located very near the borders of modern Armenia and Iran, is believed by some, especially Armenian Christians, to be the particular place where the ark came to rest and is therefore considered an especially holy place. On the basis of the Koran, however, Muslims believe Mount Cudi, located farther south (or perhaps even in Saudi Arabia), is the place of disembarkation. While there has never been any widely accepted scientific verification, some "archaeologists" claim to have found actual remains of a wooden structure, presumably Noah's ark, on Mount Ararat.

Why did Noah and his family take their voyage? Simply put, he was instructed to do so by God, who had decided to eradicate all the human family because of their wickedness. Apparently God's patience ran out when some of "the sons of God" ("angels"?) had sexual intercourse with human women and produced a race of giants (Genesis 6:1–4). God would not tolerate such behavior and determined to wipe out all living creatures by flooding the world. Noah and his family alone were to be spared because Noah was righteous in God's eyes. Noah's ark was the vehicle that enabled the continuation of the human family after a worldwide, all-encompassing divine judgment.

By now it should be clear that this is not just a straightforward account of a typical ocean voyage. The intent of this account requires a careful exploration with close attention to the context. To begin with, this biblical story has parallels in other religious traditions. Flood stories are recorded in cultures all over the globe. There is no indisputable evidence provided by *geologists* or *archaeologists* for any worldwide flood that took place at one particular time, though there is much evidence from many different places of severe flooding at various times. When these stories are found in the writings of others, they are usually recognized as myths, stories intended to disclose in some manner the ways of heavenly beings with earthly beings. These stories may be cast as history, but they are not historical. They are mythic and deal with the values that mattered to the particular people who preserved them.

The recognition that an account is not historical does not necessarily mean that it is not truthful. William Shakespeare's drama *Macbeth*, though fiction, unveils human experience in sobering and illumining ways. It is truthful, though not factual. Or consider Nelle Harper Lee's masterful novel *To Kill a Mockingbird*. The story is rich with insight into the subtleties and tragedy of racism. The setting and the characters are described so truly as to become almost real, but the truth of the work is not dependent in any way on its being historical. It is fiction, very good fiction. Literary genre is part of the context of any writing, and it must be recognized and acknowledged if interpretation is to be useful and authentic.

One particular story is of special importance here because it has so many parallels with the Noah story. The account is found in Tablet XI of a much longer story about a Mesopotamian hero named Gilgamesh. There is written evidence of this story dating back to 2500 BCE, though the complete text is found only in seventh-century BCE Assyrian documents. The Gilgamesh Epic, as it is now called, served to answer numerous questions that Mesopotamians had concerning their origins and destinies (Pritchard 1969, 72–99).

The Noah-like passage deals with a man named Utnapishtim. Like Noah, he was warned of impending disaster and instructed to construct a boat in order to escape the great flood that the gods would soon bring on the earth. Utnapishtim's vessel was totally functional, as was Noah's. The dimensions of the boat are not completely clear, but it was apparently square, rather than rectangular like Noah's, with each side 120 cubits or 200 feet long. Some think it was built as a cube—not very seaworthy, but that is not the point. It was intended to provide shelter for Utnapishtim, his family, and an unspecified number of friends and workers. And, of course, the seed of every living kind was taken on board. As the waters receded, Utnapishtim, like Noah, released a bird to see if dry land had appeared.

The existence of the Utnapishtim story has invited all manner of comparison and debate. But here the main thing to note is that in the historical context in which the Noah story was crafted there were rival accounts of how things had come to be as they were. The Noah account is certainly unique in many details, but not as a type of literature employed by people developing similar themes about the meaning of existence. Each story was told again and again because of the insights about life and the proper relationship with the divine communicated by each. The events described had occurred far away and long ago, not subject to being scientifically verified as historical. In terms of our understanding, the events were not valued as historical. But the importance of the truth to which each witnessed—at least as the preserving community understood the truth—was uncontested.

Now some Christians insist that the Noah story is historically accurate. They go to great lengths to try to demonstrate that a vessel the size of that described in Genesis would have sufficient space to house representatives of every species ever on the face of the globe. They dispute the generally accepted belief that a wooden hull much over 300 feet in length, without iron supports, would be technically difficult (probably impossible) to build, and certainly, if constructed, would be incapable of surviving anything but very placid waters for a relatively short time. Indeed, some people are at work constructing a model that they believe demonstrates the factuality of the Noah story. How they will replicate the torrent of waters described in Genesis remains to be seen.

To get snarled in the detail of the story at that level, however, is to risk missing the point of the narrative. The literary context of the story suggests other points of emphasis. The Noah account comes in the middle of the opening eleven chapters of the Bible. The whole of humankind as related to God is the concern. Categories such as "Israelite" or "Jew" are inappropriate and inaccurate as yet. The stories about Adam and Eve, Cain and Abel, and Noah share in the fact that each has to do with the whole human family. From the story's point of view no one is exempt. Everyone, every human being, has a stake.

Genesis begins by affirming that God created all that is, including humankind, and humans male and female were fashioned in the very image of God. Humans were given responsibility for the careful and faithful management of all living things. Adam and Eve, the symbolic representatives of the whole human family, were placed in a garden where the unending opportunity of life abundant in the presence of God was established. But the humans defied God and were expelled from the place of the tree of life, that is, they became mortal. According to the story in Genesis, humans were soon murdering one another and squandering the gifts of life bestowed by God.

At this point in the narrative we find the Noah account. God is so disgusted with the behavior of humans that their obliteration, by flood, is planned. But God is not quite ready to give up on the whole divine project. Noah is singled out to provide the starting point for a new humanity. Noah is described as "righteous," indicating that he truly loved and respected God, at least as compared with all others of his generation. Thus Noah becomes the leading character on the surface of the account. But the story is really about God, and about God's decision to bring judgment upon wicked human beings who have forgotten their origins and their obligations. The details of the story are intended to underscore how severe was the judgment— every living creature, all flesh, except for Noah and his family and the living things preserved by Noah, are destroyed. The earth is purged of wickedness.

But that is not the end of the story, and indeed, that is not the main point of the account in the larger literary context. The main point comes after Noah's voyage. After the great deluge God's relationship with humankind is reasserted, but under new conditions. This is the most significant aspect of the story as far as the rest of the Bible is concerned. God's judgment is devastating, but it is not the last word. Just as God had provided for Adam and Eve when they were expelled from the garden of Eden (Genesis 3), just as Cain was protected even after being judged by God (Genesis 4), so again God continues the divine project with an undeserving humankind through the righteous, but far from perfect, Noah (Genesis 6:9; 9:20–22).

When Noah left the ark, the text recounts, he prepared a great burnt offering before God (Genesis 8:20). The divine response, as the story tells it, was one of pleasure and a divine decision never again to destroy all living creatures, even though humankind, by nature or by inclination of heart, was still rebellious and evil (8:21). Two signs of divine faithfulness to this decision were given. First, the regular sequence of the seasons of the year, as well as the regular rhythm of day and night, would never be interrupted (8:22). Second, periodically, the divine decision to preserve human life would be signaled by the appearance of a rainbow (9:12–17). The Hebrew word translated as "rainbow" can also refer to a "war bow," so what is being announced could be the end of divine hostility toward the human family. Unless God had made this decision, the story of the Bible would have been over. By making this decision God demonstrated a determination to proceed with the divine project even though the human creatures, fashioned in God's own image (1:27), had defied and disappointed their Maker.

As part of God's new plan, a binding agreement (in biblical language, a "covenant") was established between God and humanity.

The rainbow was ever to remind both God and the human family of their relationship (Genesis 9:12–17). The charge God gave to humankind at the creation was given once again: "Be fruitful and multiply, and fill the earth" (1:28; 9:1, 7). Such a charge, in the context of the story, was perfectly in order. The world needed repopulating. In the contemporary world, however, where overpopulation poses a threat to the quality of life for many, the command to propagate has to be balanced with the command to be good stewards. Further, the spilling of blood, whether by an animal or a human, was strictly prohibited (9:5–6). "Blood" and "life" were intimately connected and to be respected. Violence was not to be tolerated. These were the stipulations imposed on humankind. God in return pledged never again to destroy the world by flood (9:15).

What this story means for contemporary people is not as self-evident as might at first be assumed. The application of ancient texts that come from times and places far distant requires careful examination of the differences between now and then and reflection of how now to best honor the God-given covenant. Various Christians, Jews, and Muslims have responded differently to this text. Some insist that unmanaged increase of the human species is still God's desire. Others argue that Noah's circumstance and that of the world today are totally different. Thus it is inhumane and irresponsible to encourage, or allow by inaction, the rapid growth of population, especially as is happening in some "underdeveloped" countries. Some make a case for capital punishment on the basis of this text. Others point out that there is a severe contradiction in a text that says no life is to be taken and then turns around and insists that a life must be given for a life taken. Ancient religious texts do still have an impact on those who read them as scripture, but it is not always uniform or predictable.

Another kind of response to this story stresses that this is not a tribal story. God's covenant with Noah, the "Noachian covenant" as it is called, is made with the representative of the whole human family. Indeed, Noah's three sons, Shem, Ham, and Japheth, were considered the eponyms of every known people in the world. (Though some have argued otherwise, Native Americans and Asians were not included because they were unknown to the crafters of the tradition.) The importance of Noah is as representative of all human beings, not as someone only one group might claim as theirs. God's concern for the whole human family is the point of the narrative, as the literary context so ably insists. God desires to begin again in the effort to establish the proper relationship between the human and divine, the relationship lost as a result of human wickedness.

In the Babylonian story the hero Utnapishtim is granted immortality after the flood but is exiled to a distant place where he can have no contact with any other mortal except his wife. In the biblical story a different plot is developed. Noah plunges right back into a very mortal existence. The people with whom God will continue to interact are not semidivine, perfect people. They are real human beings with real human foibles. Noah's experience was not even a great learning event for the human family—in the story that follows foolish, arrogant humans try to assault the heavens by building the tower of Babel (Genesis 11). But the story reports that a highly significant change came about in God's heart. God decided to begin again and to employ whatever was necessary to achieve the divine purpose while respecting a certain degree of human autonomy. The great debate concerning the extent of human free will began with the events in the garden of Eden and is continued with the outcome of Noah's cruise.

God, of course, could have dealt with the problem of human wickedness by creating a whole new humanity, starting from scratch. Or God might have left humans out of the new creation altogether and fashioned some other creature that would have been more faithfully and joyfully responsible. God might have shipped Noah and his family to some far distant paradise, as happened with Utnapishtim, and ended the story there, allowing for no new human family and no relationship with God. God probably had even more options than those imagined so far, but the account as we have it pushes in a much different direction.

The biblical writer asserts that God chose to work with Noah and his family, humans with all manner of frailties, faults, and limitations. God chose to continue in relationship with these humans and to enter into covenant with them. God chose to signal the universal character of the covenant with the rainbow, a reappearing, visible sign testifying to divine care. Finally, God announced that there would be no future cruises of the sort Noah had taken because God would never again deal with wickedness by sending a flood to destroy humanity.

What do we learn about God from this account? Several things are worthy of note and emphasis. The first eleven chapters of Genesis are about God's relationship with humanity, with all human beings. This story may be found in the book Christians call the Old (or First) Testament, a book known by other names by Jews and Muslims but revered no less. But the message is that God's concerns go well beyond any one people or any one religion. There are no Jews, Christians, or Muslims, identified as such, in this story, only human beings. The flood affects the whole human family. The whole human family is delivered because Noah at God's instruction takes a very unlikely journey. This story emphasizes the universal extent of God's concern. The circle of divine love is wide.

Noah's account also presents God as one willing to change course and take risks. God was appalled at what was happening on earth. That was what prompted the decision to flood the world. God was sorry for even creating human beings and decided to rectify the situation. But God also deeply desired a positive relationship with humanity. So God decided to take a chance with Noah and try again. Indeed, as the story in Genesis continues, we find that God had to start over repeatedly and had to employ ever-changing strategies. God was prepared to risk frustration and disappointment. The point is that God, as pictured in the Bible, is willing to adjust to new circumstances while keeping the divine goal in view.

Finally, the aftermath of Noah's cruise, the covenant that God established, makes a very important statement in the opening pages of the Bible. The God the Bible presents, in a rich variety of ways, is a God of grace as well as power. With the new beginning inaugurated after the deliverance of Noah and his family by the placing of God's bow in the heavens, God makes clear that the divine intention is directed toward all human beings, not only some. God's justice and love are extended to and include all people, not only the people of the Book, namely Jews, Christians, and Muslims. Though the Bible recounts God's actions and concerns in relation to particular individuals and particular groups who lived in particular places at particular times, the central actor of the overall drama, namely

God, remains the God of all humanity who maintains a very wide-reaching agenda.

Like the ripples caused by a pebble tossed into a pond—perhaps like those of an ark launched on an incredible voyage—God's love, the Bible suggests, has been rippling forth across the pool of humanity at least since the time of Noah. This love is the Bible's main concern. This love, God's love, provides the ongoing impetus for reaching out to others just as God has reached out to humanity. In Noah's story the rainbow becomes the sign to all God's creatures of the wideness of God's unending and all-embracing love.

Chapter Five

A Long Way from Ur

*T*erah was a Mesopotamian reputed to have lived around four thousand years ago in a place named Ur. Terah is significant for our consideration because of his son Abram (who became Abraham), who is held in high esteem by the followers of three of the world's great religions, Judaism, Christianity, and Islam. It is the tradition associated with Abraham that will be considered here because, as with Noah, God's love is made manifest in the life of a non-Israelite, a non-Christian, a non-Muslim.

Ur was located in what is now Iraq, about two hundred miles southeast of Baghdad and one hundred miles northwest of the border with Kuwait, on the banks of the Euphrates River. The site has been excavated in modern times and has yielded significant artifacts, including a number of clay tablets with cuneiform writing. Ur was an important city in the time of the Sumerian civilization (roughly 3500–2000 BCE) with an estimated population of around thirty thousand at its height. The moon god named Nanna (later called Sin), was believed to be the primary divine protector of the city. A debate continues to this day between Muslims and non-Muslims on whether or how Allah is to be related to the deity revered in ancient Ur.

According to Genesis 11:27–32, Terah had three sons named Abram, Nahor, and Haran. The degree of historicity of the account is debated, but the story reflects what is known of Mesopotamia at around 2000–1900 BCE. Terah set out from Ur for the land of Canaan. Perhaps there was an economic downturn in Ur or political upheaval or war or plague. Maybe Terah just had an adventurous side and liked to travel. Perhaps there was some form of major environmental change. Or again, the death of his son Haran that is noted in the text may simply have made Ur an unhappy place for Terah (Genesis 11:28). At any rate, he left Ur and took with him his family, Abram with his wife Sarai, Nahor and his wife Milcah, and his grandson Lot, Haran's son, and possibly other unnamed family and servants.

Terah headed for Canaan, approximately one thousand miles away at the other side of the Fertile Crescent. He no doubt followed established trade routes that linked east and west, but it was not like hopping in the SUV and heading down the interstate. The Fertile Crescent was (and still is) the arch of land that extends from the mouth of the Tigris and Euphrates Rivers up to what is now southern Turkey and then down along the Mediterranean Sea, through and including parts of modern Syria, Lebanon, and Israel/Palestine, to Egypt. At the time when Terah may have lived, the Fertile Crescent, with Egypt, encompassed for Mesopotamians the whole of the known civilized world. Terah intended to journey from the far eastern side to the far western side of the crescent, from one side of his world to the other, a very long journey indeed, a long way from Ur.

At least according to the story, Terah did not make it to Canaan. He made it only as far as Haran, a city located in what is now southeastern Turkey, about seven hundred miles north of Ur. It was coincidental (or was it?) that the name of the city was the same as that of the lost son. Archaeological work has recovered some materials from Haran, but there are not sufficient data to estimate the size of the population. Haran is mentioned as a thriving city in writings found among some eighty thousand tablets excavated at Ebla (Tell Mardikh), located in modern Syria a few miles south of Aleppo. As in Ur, the moon god Sin was considered the primary deity protecting and caring for the city. In Haran Terah and his family settled and apparently prospered. Some time later Terah's son Abram left to complete the trek to Canaan. Abram took with him "all the possessions they had gathered, and the persons whom they had acquired in Haran" (Genesis 12:5).

Now in Genesis, and the rest of the Bible for that matter, Abram (who becomes Abraham), not Terah, is the important figure in this narrative. But Abram had a history before he reached Canaan, and that is of some significance for the rest of the story. Terah and his family, including Abram, were not Jews or Israelites or Canaanites. Nor were they Palestinians or Christians or Muslims. They were Mesopotamians, Urites, and later Haranians. As far as we know, they shared the worldview, including the religious perceptions, of the people around them. They were neither better nor worse, religiously speaking, than their neighbors. As far as the narrative is concerned, Abram was a Mesopotamian, a pagan, who became a participant in a divine reality show that evolved into what we know as the Bible.

The biblical story of Abram/Abraham is preserved primarily in Genesis 12–24. By one read, Abraham comes off looking rather bad. Bruce Feiler summarized the story in his bestseller, *Abraham: A Journey to the Heart of Three Faiths,* in these words:

> He [Abraham] has no mother. He has no past. He has no personality. The man who will redefine the world appears suddenly, almost as an afterthought, with no trumpet fanfare, no fluttering doves, in Genesis 11, verse 26: "When Terah had lived seventy years, he became the father of Abram, Nahor, and Haran." From this a-heroic start, Abram (the name in Hebrew means "the father is exalted" or "mighty father") goes on to abandon his father at age seventy-five, leave his homeland, move to Canaan, travel to Egypt, father two sons, change his name, cut off part of his penis, do the same for his teenager and newborn, exile his first son, attempt to kill his second, fight a world war, buy some land, bury his wife, father another family, and die at one hundred seventy-five. (Feiler 2002, 18–19)

But, of course, the real significance of Abraham lies as much between the lines as at the surface of the narrative, a point that Feiler's work illustrates well.

The biblical narrative is shaped around a divine promise, a commitment that God initiated without any apparent reason. Out of the blue, so to speak, God's word came to Abram. Did the Lord actually speak to him like we might talk with one another over coffee, or is this simply a literary device, a way to talk about things that in the final regard cannot be reduced to observable behavior? Probably the latter. This text is not to be read as empirically factual. But the point is clear.

The Lord instituted a relationship centered upon a divine directive and promise. Thus Abram became "the father—in many cases, the purported *biological* father—of 12 million Jews, 2 billion Christians, and 1 billion Muslims around the world. He is history's first monotheist" (Feiler 2002, 9). Because God fashioned this special relationship with Abram, the former Urite, Abram's place in the Bible is secure. He alone is remembered as the "friend of God" (Isaiah 41:8; 2 Chronicles 20:7; James 2:23).

The Lord, according to Genesis 12:1, instructed Abram to leave Haran and all his kindred to go at divine direction to a land initially unidentified. Further, Abram received a promise:

> I will make of you a great nation, and I will bless you, and make your name great, so that you will be a blessing. I will bless those who bless you, and the one who curses you I will curse; and in you all the families of the earth shall be blessed. (Genesis 12:2–3)

Later in the story this promise is reiterated and sealed with a covenant (Genesis 17:1–22). Numerous progeny are assured to Abram and Sarai, who are renamed Abraham (in Hebrew "father of multitudes") and Sarah (a variant form of Sarai). The covenant assured Abraham and Sarah of God's commitment to continue the promise to the generations of their offspring to follow and the gift of "all the land of Canaan, for a perpetual holding" (17:8). The rite of circumcision became the sign of this divinely instituted agreement (17:10–14).

The account of Abraham's journeys with Sarah illustrates how this promise was actualized as they continued toward Terah's original destination, Canaan, such a long way from Ur. In the New Testament book of Hebrews, Abraham is praised as a man of consummate faith (Hebrews 11:8–19). Certainly in hindsight such an accolade is appropriate. But in Genesis there seems to have been as much uncertainty (doubt?) as trust on the part of the patriarch and matriarch.

Two episodes illustrate this well. Each involves Abraham and Sarah in the court of a king. The first account comes immediately after the Lord initiated the new relationship of promise (Genesis 12:10–20). The narrative is situated at the court of an unnamed pharaoh of Egypt. Abraham was afraid that the king would want his beautiful wife Sarah for his harem and kill Abraham in order to take her as his own. Out of fear (but what about the divine promise?) Abraham asked Sarah to say she was his sister. She did, and Pharaoh took her, and Abraham was left unharmed. God, however, was displeased and responded by sending plagues on Pharaoh. The Egyptian king recognized the divine rebuke and in turn called Abraham on the carpet for having deceived him into a potentially adulterous relationship with Sarah. Sarah was immediately released and Pharaoh sent Abraham and his entourage on their way.

The second account is strikingly similar (Genesis 20:1–17). This time Abraham and Sarah are in Gerar, a city located somewhere, as yet unidentified, in the Negev, the southern desert of Palestine. Abimelech is the king. After taking Sarah, whom Abraham identified as his sister rather than wife, Abimelech was warned by God in a dream of Abraham's deception and of impending disaster if Abimelech consummated the adulterous union. The king strongly reprimanded Abraham for lying to him. Then, along with abundant gifts, Abimelech restored Sarah to Abraham and allowed them to settle wherever they chose in his land.

Neither of these stories presents Abraham as particularly trusting of God. In consideration of the divine promise of intended blessing, why was Abraham so fearful? Of course, from a human point of view it is quite sensible. Abraham and Sarah were strangers journeying through countries not their own. They were a long way from Ur and it was natural to feel threatened. But probably even in Ur it was not considered virtuous for a husband to trade his wife for personal safety. Even more to the point, Sarah was to be the mother of the progeny promised by God, but how could this happen if she was made part of a royal harem?

On the other hand, Pharaoh and King Abimelech are presented as God-fearing, moral rulers. Their absolute power to do whatever they willed was moderated by their ethical sensitivity. They had moral standards that prohibited, among other things, lying, stealing, and adultery. They knew that divine authority circumscribed their royal power. They are not described as being in covenant with the Lord God, but they are attentive and responsive to divine intervention. In the narrative plot, each of the kings stands as a reminder that God, almost in spite of Abraham and Sarah, will be the one who sees the divine project to fulfillment. Neither God's love nor influence is limited to Abraham and Sarah. God has other sheep too, namely Pharaoh and Abimelech.

Abraham's lack of confidence in the divine promise is evidenced in two other ways as well. In Genesis 15:2 we learn that since God had not yet provided Abraham and Sarah with a child, Abraham named Eliezer of Damascus as his heir. This Eliezer may be the trusted servant mentioned in 24:2, though this is not certain. It was the custom for someone who had no heir by birth to adopt someone else, making that person legally an heir. Not infrequently a trusted servant was chosen. Whether Abraham's words indicate that he actually adopted Eliezer so he could be his heir is uncertain. Perhaps he was merely expressing himself in words of exaggerated frustration because an heir had not yet been born. In either instance, the episode reveals Abraham's efforts to take his future into his own hands, to fulfill God's promise in his own way. For the plot of the narrative it is hardly accidental that immediately following Abraham's declaration, the writer of Genesis presents a second announcement of God's promise. This time the commitment is expressed even more forcefully and punctuated with a dramatic sacrificial ceremony where God pledges, even at the risk of personal destruction, to fulfill the divine commitment (15:12–21).

As if this were not enough, according to the Bible, Sarah decided to become proactive in bringing God's promise to fruition. Sarah knew what God should be doing, namely providing an heir through whom the promise could be realized (Genesis 16). But the normal process for such an outcome seemed impossible: Sarah was barren. This was noted at the very outset of the narrative (Genesis 11:30). Thus, since she continued to be childless (16:2), Sarah decided to have Abraham impregnate her Egyptian slave-girl Hagar. Any child born of such a union would, by custom, be understood as Sarah's child. Were the child a son, then, the long desired, but not yet present, heir would be provided. Such a legal tradition has been documented in tablets dating from around 1600–1500 BCE, found in Nuzi, a site located in what is now northeastern Iraq. As the story tells us, Abraham did have intercourse with Hagar, and Ishmael was born. Thereby a legal heir was born to Abraham.

Now this was all fine and good, but it left God out of the picture. Sarah's plan, like Abraham's, was just one more indication that neither she nor Abraham really believed that God could or would break through Sarah's barrenness. Rather than live in trust, Abraham and Sarah took matters into their own hands. They unfaithfully arranged for the birth of their own heir, Ishmael. But this was not the way God intended things to go. Ishmael did grow up to be the father of a great people. Indeed, Ishmael is as important for contemporary Muslims as Isaac is for Jews and Christians. But it was through Isaac, the second son fathered by Abraham, the only son born to Sarah, that, according to the biblical story, the divine promise was passed (Genesis 21).

It is Isaac, the second son, who is at the center of what is certainly the most dramatic scene in the whole Abraham story. This extraordinary episode, involving Abraham, Isaac, and God, is recounted in Genesis 22. In Jewish tradition this event is called, in Hebrew, the *akedah,* or in English, the "binding" of Isaac. Christians refer to the episode as "the sacrifice of Isaac." For Muslims, an event strikingly similar is recorded in sura 37 of the Koran involving Abraham and Ishmael. This is known in Arabic as the *dhabih* and is commemorated as part of the great *hajj* held annually at Mecca. While Islamic tradition originally acknowledged this story as being about Isaac, in later centuries Ishmael was identified as the son who accompanied Abraham to the place of sacrifice.

Genesis 22 recounts how God instructed Abraham to take his beloved son Isaac to a distant place, the land of Moriah, and offer him as a burnt offering. In terms of historical or archaeological evidence, the location of Moriah is unclear, but by tradition Moriah came to be associated with Jerusalem. The Muslim holy place, Haram al-Sharif (the Dome of the Rock), built between 687 and 691 CE, is believed to stand over the place. Jewish tradition holds that Solomon's Temple had previously stood on the spot, and of course Christians believe that Jesus often visited the Temple of Herod that stood there in his lifetime.

In the story Isaac is referred to repeatedly as Abraham's only son, the son Abraham loves. Isaac was the son of promise, the sign of God's commitment. Nonetheless, Abraham took Isaac and went forth obediently to carry out the divine instruction. What were his feelings?

What was Isaac thinking? The story is silent. Thankfully, however, at the very moment Abraham was poised with knife in hand to kill Isaac, an angel of the Lord intervened and halted Abraham. A ram was found tangled in nearby brush. The angel instructed Abraham to substitute the ram for Isaac, his beloved son. Thus Isaac was spared. Abraham, finally, had demonstrated absolute trust in God. Abraham no longer would try to take things into his own hands. As a result, Abraham became the model for trusting faithfulness.

Interpreters have often pointed out that this was *God's* test of Abraham. God would never have allowed Isaac to become a human sacrifice. God's aim was to test Abraham's mettle, so to speak, to see whether he had yet developed adequate trust in God's capacity to ensure the divine promise. Up to this point in the story, neither Abraham nor Sarah had demonstrated especially noteworthy trust in God. Thus the story should be read with this in mind. It is also to be noted that, while human sacrifice was practiced across the centuries by various peoples of the ancient world, on the basis of this story later Hebrew tradition castigated all who perpetrated such practice. In ancient Israel legitimate forms of sacrificial offering could involve only animals, birds, and grain.

While this may be true, the terror evoked by the story is still real. This is not bedtime reading for the family. To emphasize a story where a father becomes a model for religious devotion because he is willing to kill a beloved child certainly raises questions. This cannot go without notice. This kind of text can become a source for a form of religious zeal that can yield terrible fruit. Religious devotion is worthy, but obedience to God must be measured with a moral sensitivity that acknowledges that every human being is created in the divine image and is thereby treasured by God. Militant religious extremism is not the aim of this passage.

This story about Abraham and Isaac has horrified and astonished people down through the generations that have preserved it. Thankfully, though long after the biblical period, a positive spin on this dramatic account did emerge. Feiler reports the legend in this way:

> Immediately after the boy is saved, he lies on the altar, clutching the knife, the emotion of the ordeal flooding from his body. God

tells him he will grant him any prayer. "O God, I pray that you grant me this," the boy says. "When any person in any era meets you at the gates of Heaven—whether they believe in you or not—I ask that you allow them to enter Paradise." (Feiler 2002, 108–9)

Genesis 22 may have been intended to laud Abraham's obedience, but it is easy to see how it can be misunderstood with tragic consequences. Adherents of all three Abrahamic faiths have, at times, used the story about Abraham and Isaac to justify various forms of religious fanaticism. The legend of Isaac's prayer warns against any such misuse of the tradition. Blessing, not curse, is the divine goal.

The story is primarily about God's reliability, not Abraham's obedience. Yes, God did want to see if Abraham had yet learned that God's promises were trustworthy, but it should not be forgotten that the God who tested Abraham was also the one who had provided Isaac in the first place. The main point of the story, in the literary context in which it is found, is that finally Abraham does come to understand the total sufficiency and trustworthiness of God. It is in this sense that Abraham is rightly praised in the New Testament for his faithfulness (Hebrews 11:8–20).

As I mentioned with the story about Noah, it is imperative to note the historical and literary contexts. There is no conclusive way to date the formation of the Abraham-Sarah stories. Some of the episodes contain hints of their great antiquity. But other clues suggest that the story was given its final shape no earlier than the seventh century BCE. Perhaps one such clue can suffice to illustrate the point. The phrase "Ur of the Chaldeans" could not have been written with meaning before the Chaldeans occupied the territory where Ur was most likely situated. That took place historically in the late seventh century. Thus the completed Genesis account as it is found in the Bible was written sometime after the seventh century BCE.

This is significant. It reminds us that while some, maybe even many, of the traditions about Abraham and Sarah may have great antiquity, they were most likely gathered and arranged in the form preserved in the Bible much later than the time of the events remembered. Many scholars believe that the final literary shaping of the Abrahamic tradition took place after the Babylonians had destroyed

Judah and Solomon's Temple in Jerusalem, and taken many Judahites into captivity in Babylonia in 587 BCE. Thus the shaping of the narrative occurred over a thousand years after the period in which the story is set.

Whatever the original meaning of some of the traditions, the narrative as a whole takes on new meaning during and after the Babylonian exile in the sixth century BCE. This story about a family seeking to follow God through uncharted territory clearly had special importance for people deported from their homeland as they wondered whether God cared about them and was sufficient for the challenges they faced. Modern readers face the same challenge in adapting the ancient story to speak a new word in a different time.

It is also significant that Abraham and Sarah appear in the Bible *before* Moses, who is indisputably revered as the founder of Judaism (though technically that term cannot be used to describe modern Judaism until after the second or third century CE). As with Noah, God's project is still directed at the whole human family. To be sure, Abraham will stand at the head of the lineage that will include, in the Bible, David and Jesus, and in the Koran, Muhammad as well. Jews, Christians, and Muslims will claim Abraham and Sarah/Hagar as their figurative parents, at least, and perhaps for some as the biological source of their very DNA.

But as the story is presented in the Bible, God's dealings with Abraham and Sarah do not yet represent the divine decision to relate with humanity through a chosen people. That will come after Moses. In the stories in Genesis the horizon is wider. With Abraham God is pictured working through an Urite in a land far distant from this Mesopotamian's land of birth. Though Abraham did buy land for Sarah's burial place in Hebron, located some thirty miles south of Jerusalem (Genesis 24:2), he was always considered, at best, a resident alien by those among whom he lived in Canaan. He remained an Urite or, at best, a Haranian. He did not even begin with a religious connection to the God who would be so closely identified with him and his progeny as the God of Abraham, Isaac, and Jacob.

Not a Jew, Christian, or Muslim, at least as Genesis tells it, Abraham was an unlikely Mesopotamian through whom God chose to continue the divine project of refashioning the whole human family. God's agenda of gracious, creative love was made concrete in Abraham and his family for the sake of the families of the earth. By the end of this story, Abraham had certainly come a long way from Ur, both geographically and theologically. Symbolically or metaphorically speaking, the wideness of God's mercy and love is established and stands as the basis on which the rest of the Bible is to be interpreted.

Chapter Six

Only a Whistle Away

*T*imes were tough back in '35. Mismanagement and greed had scandalized the nation and brought collapse to the financial markets. The economy was in shambles. Particularly in the cities were the hard times felt. The judicial system lacked integrity. On the international front new powers were flexing their muscles. There were reports of impending war, evidence of emerging military capabilities on a scale beyond previous experience, rumors of the possibility of unspeakable atrocities. The political and religious leaders were uncertain of what to do, and so most did nothing. There were many reasons for a sense of helplessness and hopelessness. Whistling in the dark was probably becoming an art. Yes, things were bad in Judah back in the year 735 BCE, a time somewhat like the present. As with the present, part of the issue concerns how God is to be understood as relating (if at all) to the messy and very diverse particularities of history.

Judah was a small nation located in southern Canaan, part of the piece of geography that the Romans much later named Palestine. Judah had for about eighty years been part of a larger nation called Israel founded by King David back in the tenth century BCE. The united monarchy, as biblical historians call it, wracked by dissension, divided in 922 BCE into two nations, with one called Israel situated in the north and the other, Judah, occupying the south. The dynasty started by David son of Jesse continued in power through over four hundred years of Judah's history, which ended with the destruction of the nation by Babylonia in 587 BCE. In 735 BCE, when a man named Ahaz was king of Judah, Judah confronted the greatest set of threats to its security and prosperity since the breakup of the united monarchy nearly two hundred years earlier. In the midst of this uncertainty a man named Isaiah son of Amoz stepped forward. Not a great deal is known about his personal life. He lived in Jerusalem with his wife, whom he called "the prophetess" (Isaiah 8:3). They had two sons, each of whom bore symbolic names that reflected prophetic oracles proclaimed to the people of Judah (7:3; 8:3). One was called Shear-jashub (Hebrew for "a remnant shall return"). The other was named Maher-shalal-hash-baz (Hebrew for "the spoil speeds, the prey hastens"). Later tradition understood Isaiah to be a nephew of the Judean king Amaziah, who reigned in the early decades of the eighth century BCE. Whether he had any family connection with the royal house or not, he did seem to have access to King Ahaz (742–727 BCE) and King Hezekiah (727–698 BCE) during the course of their reigns. Isaiah may have also had a third son with the symbolic name Immanuel (Hebrew for "God is with us"), though this boy may have been born to Hezekiah, according to some scholars (7:14; 8:8). The name is important to Christians because it was claimed in reference to Jesus.

Isaiah's job was being a prophet. He began work "in the year that King Uzziah died" (Isaiah 6:1), probably 742 BCE. There were other prophets before him, notably Moses, Elijah, Elisha, Micaiah, Amos, and Hosea. Another prophet named Micah was a contemporary. There were probably many other men and women who served in this capacity whose names and words were not preserved. Contrary to popular opinion, predicting the future was not their primary business. They did not have radio or TV shows on which they tried to prove that 9/11 had been predicted centuries earlier. They were not in the business of trying to predict when the world would come to an end or when the Lord might execute final judgment. The future in that sense was simply not their concern. Sure, sometimes they did have a word from the Lord about what God intended to do down the road, but almost always such future pictures were painted in broad strokes rather than in date-specific detail. Mostly, present time was the major concern of the prophets. What were people doing now? Was the king doing what he was expected to do according to divine ordinance? Were people dealing with one another humanely and justly? Were the courts maintaining justice? *Now* was mostly the focus.

The prophets' job was to make clear God's expectations, first to the kings and then to the people, in terms of maintaining a just society geared especially at protecting the most vulnerable citizens. When the king or people failed to live according to God's commands and teaching, then the prophets announced impending punishment with the hope of bringing about repentance and behavior that would be pleasing to God. Isaiah spent over forty years at this task, though with only occasional success. He walked around Jerusalem naked for three years trying to make a point (Isaiah 20). Did he go off to work each day happily whistling? Probably not. Nonetheless, his message rang true, and disciples preserved at least some of his words (8:16).

These pronouncements form the core of the biblical book named after Isaiah, though the book as it now stands contains much more than only the words of Isaiah of Jerusalem. Across the centuries a number of other prophets and poets expounded on Isaiah's work, adding their own "words of the LORD" to those of Isaiah. Thus the biblical book has material dating from as early as 742 BCE down to possibly as late as the 300s BCE. Many different literary and historical contexts are encountered reflecting this nearly four-hundred-year history. There is often no clear signal to help recognize changes in historical context or literary genre. Thus there is no way, in short compass, to do justice to the rich content of this amazingly complex book.

Still, a number of themes well worth consideration inform an understanding of this prophet's perception. Isaiah's perception of God is inspiring, certainly nothing to sneeze at. Perhaps the place to begin is with Isaiah's inaugural vision, also known as his "call" (Isaiah 6). Isaiah's experience apparently took place in the temple. Isaiah caught only a glimpse of God, actually only the hem of the Divine King's robe that "filled the temple" (6:1). The immediate result for Isaiah was an overwhelming sense of his own guilt and unworthiness, followed by an act of divine cleansing (6:5–7). The remainder of the passage spells out the rather gloomy mission accepted by Isaiah to announce God's impending judgment on Judah (6:8–13).

At the very outset of the vision, however, are important words ascribed to some form of "angel-like" heavenly beings called "seraphs" (in Hebrew, *seraphim*). The etymology of the term "seraph" suggests something fiery and serpentlike, but not a great deal is reported about these creatures. Their task seems to have been to guard the divine throne from the approach of anyone or anything unworthy. Isaiah reported hearing them call to one another: "Holy, holy, holy is the LORD of hosts; the whole earth is full of his glory" (Isaiah 6:3). The words of the seraphs became defining for the prophet's understanding of God.

Expressed in these words are two key insights. First, God is holy. For the ancient Hebrews this meant that God was totally other, not defined by human limitations, and totally pure, unsullied by sin, uncontaminated by the unclean, so clearly a part of human experience. The Holy One stood beyond all that was human. But at the same time, and the second affirmation of the seraphs, God's glory filled the earth. The term "glory" (in Hebrew, *kabod*) was used most frequently in connection with the tabernacle in the wilderness or with the Temple built by Solomon in Jerusalem. The *kabod* had a fiery, shiny glow that became the very symbol of divine presence. God's *kabod* rested on the tabernacle and filled the Temple. What is remarkable here is that Isaiah recognized that the whole earth was filled with God's glory, the divine *kabod*. Israel's God was present among all people and had a stake in the whole world.

Though Isaiah directed his words to a very particular, historical people, a people in covenant with the Lord who had delivered the Hebrews from bondage in Egypt, Isaiah viewed God as king of the whole world. Isaiah was sent to reprimand and call to repentance Judahites who lived over twenty-seven hundred years ago, but his word was not limited to them nor was the God to whom Isaiah witnessed limited. There was no place in the world nor any people in the world who stood beyond the realm of the Holy One, whose glory filled the whole earth. God's love could flow freely wherever and whenever directed by God.

The all-embracing relationship of God with the human family began at creation and was reconfirmed with Noah. The story was advanced by Abraham, Sarah, and Hagar. In Isaiah this theme is articulated in two other ways. One is negative and the other positive. The negative side has to do with divine judgment. Much of Isaiah of Jerusalem's message dealt with impending disaster due to the wickedness and lack of trust in God evidenced by the king and among the people. The people took comfort in claiming that the Lord was on their side, in rejoicing because of Immanuel, "God is with us." But because God's glory was so near, and in light of the unrepentant disdain for God's ways, God's purifying judgment was also near at hand. God held the Judahites responsible for their deeds. As had prophets before him, Isaiah made clear the consequences. For a wicked people, Immanuel was bad, not good, news.

What was happening between God and the chosen people centered in Jerusalem, God's judgment, was also viewed as including the nations beyond Judah. God was going to judge Assyria, Egypt, Moab, Edom, and others of Judah's neighbors as well (Isaiah 13–23). The prophet Amos, who addressed the northern kingdom, Israel, in approximately 750 BCE had made the same assertion. God cared about the behavior of all peoples, not just the people of Israel or Judah. God held all people responsible for their actions (Amos 1–2). Though this is negative in the sense that it is about divine punishment of wrongdoing, nonetheless it assumes that God is the God of all peoples and is not the possession of any one people alone.

On the positive side, God cared for the well-being of the surrounding peoples as well. Near the beginning of the book of Isaiah there is a very significant announcement (Isaiah 2:1–4). The message is paralleled in the words of another prophet who lived at the same time as Isaiah of Jerusalem, Micah of Moresheth (Micah 4:1–4). Perhaps each prophet drew upon a tradition circulated among the prophets. Isaiah envisioned a time when God would establish peace throughout the world. The Lord would secure justice and order among the nations for the benefit of all peoples. Jerusalem would be elevated and recognized as the place to go for instruction in God's ways. The promise given to Abraham and Sarah that the nations of the world would be blessed through them would be realized fully. In the midst of a book centered on God's dealings with the chosen people, this introductory announcement colors the whole context in which Isaiah's words are to be heard.

There is one further aspect of Isaiah's understanding of God's relationship with the people outside the circle of the chosen. Isaiah considered them to be at the beck and call of the Holy One. They were not required to believe in the Holy One or to do homage. They belonged to God and God could direct them as necessary. God had only to whistle to bring Assyria into action as the divine agent of Judah's punishment (Isaiah 5:26–30; 7:18; 10:5–6). The Assyrians will themselves be punished for their arrogance, but first they execute God's punishment of Judah (10:7–11). Another prophet, Jeremiah, roughly a century later, understood King Nebuchadnezzar of Babylon in the same way. Perhaps most surprising of all, in the midst of the portion of Isaiah that dates from the sixth century BCE, the Persian king Cyrus, who overthrew Babylonian domination and allowed the captives from Judah to return home, is called God's "shepherd" and the Lord's "anointed" (in Hebrew, *mashiach,* also translated "messiah"; 44:28; 45:1). God directs the rulers of the world, including the most feared of enemies, and God will bring all peoples—including but not limited to the chosen—both to judgment and to restoration.

At least one other theme warrants consideration. It appears most often in what is known among scholars as the exilic Isaiah, namely Isaiah 40–66. The historical context of the later chapters of the book of Isaiah is during and after the time of the Babylonian exile. In 587 BCE after Judah was totally destroyed by Nebuchadnezzar, a number of people were taken captive to Babylonia. They were kept there until 538 when Cyrus the Persian, who had defeated the Babylonians in 539, offered the opportunity to return to Judah. Some accepted the opportunity, but many remained in Babylonia and began a community that some six centuries later would mold and preserve one of the most influential collections of traditions, the Babylonian Talmud. The Talmud preserves a vast body of rabbinic interpretation of the Bible and other traditions and historical lore. The Babylonian Talmud remains until this day a primary source for Jewish reflection and definition. From the time of exile many sources of tradition were shaped and preserved, including, as already noted, the accounts of Noah and Abraham. For Isaiah of Jerusalem the incursion of Assyria provided the backdrop. For the prophet of the exile, Babylon and Persia were the empires within which the survivors of Judah sought understanding of and direction from the Holy One.

During the exile, concerns about God as creator became particularly important. In Babylon the god Marduk was celebrated annually as the creator and ruler of the world. This New Year's Festival coincided with the vernal equinox in the spring of each year. With elaborate ceremony Marduk's statue was paraded through the city. The *Enuma elish* (Pritchard 1969, 60–72), the Babylonian version of the creation of the world, was recited before Marduk, and his authority over all other deities was reaffirmed. In the Babylonian creation story, and in the various Mesopotamian traditions that preceded it, the world is created from the carcass of the slain sea goddess named Tiamat. Hints of this myth show up in the Bible in references to a cosmic conflict between God and a chaos dragon named Rahab or Leviathan that God slays in the process of bringing about and maintaining an ordered world (Isaiah 27:1; 51:1; Psalm 89:10).

No doubt the Babylonian New Year's Festival made a big impression upon the Judahite captives when they first arrived in Babylon. But the Babylonian claims did not go unanswered for long. The Holy One of Israel was the only deity worthy of exaltation as Creator of the world. God's magnificent act of creation was articulated clearly and simply and placed at the very beginning of the traditions brought together to form what is now the Torah or Pentateuch, the first five books of the Bible. Genesis 1:1–2:4a offers a beautiful articulation of the power and purpose of God. The world is created at the word of God, with each step made deliberately and orderly. Humans are created in God's image as the culminating act of God's work, and then all are mandated to rest with the inauguration of the Sabbath. This account of creation is a far cry from the bloody tale told of Marduk.

Parallel to the shaping of the Genesis story, the unnamed exilic prophet whose work is preserved in Isaiah proclaimed the same message of God's creative power and energy. The emphasis was on the incomparable capacity of the Holy One of Israel to fashion the heavens and the earth. No idol (not even that of the great Marduk?) can be favorably compared with the true Creator, the Holy One of Israel (Isaiah 40:18–20). What's more, even the most powerful of nations is not to be thought of as in any way comparable to God. As the exilic Isaiah proclaimed, "Even the nations are like a drop from a bucket, and as dust on the scales. . . . All the nations are as nothing before him; they are accounted by him as less than nothing and emptiness" (40:15, 17). The magnificent poem that stands near the beginning of the exilic materials (Isaiah 40–66) concludes with these powerful and moving words:

> Have you not known? Have you not heard?
> The LORD is the everlasting God,
>   the Creator of the ends of the earth.
> He does not faint or grow weary;
>   his understanding is unsearchable.
> He gives power to the faint,
>   and strengthens the powerless.
> Even youths will faint and be weary,
>   and the young will fall exhausted;
> but those who wait for the LORD shall renew their strength,
>   they shall mount up with wings like eagles,
> they shall run and not be weary,
>   they shall walk and not faint.
>   Isaiah 40:28–31

God is the source and maintainer of all that is, Creator and Lord!

God's power as Creator, for the exilic prophet in Isaiah, parallels another important claim about God. The Holy One of Israel is the creator of all and therefore rightly claims dominion over the whole world. At the same time, the Holy One of Israel, whose glory fills the earth, is proclaimed redeemer of Israel and the nations. Cyrus the Persian, as noted earlier, was the human political agent that enabled the captives of Judah to return to their homeland. There was also an unidentified but loyal servant of the Lord who had a crucial role in the deliverance that was announced (Isaiah 42:1–9). Some argue that this servant was none other than the prophet. Others contend the servant was Israel as a community or at least some portion of the people who had remained faithful to God throughout the ordeal of captivity. The New Testament saw in the description of this servant a portrait of Jesus (for instance, see Matthew 12:15–21; 1 Peter 1:21–25). But whoever the servant was and whatever the role exercised by Cyrus, the prophet made clear: in the final analysis, the Holy One of Israel, the Creator whose glory fills the earth, alone was to receive the praise for orchestrating the overthrow of Babylon and the redemption of the exiles (Isaiah 48).

In the historical context from which the book of Isaiah comes, it is not at all surprising that God was understood as deeply concerned about Judah as the concrete manifestation of Israel, the special people of God. God's holy, demanding, cleansing love was directed through Isaiah, and by those other prophets who followed in Isaiah's tradition, to a particular audience who lived in a concrete place and time. Thus the message met the people where they were.

What is remarkable, however, is that from beginning to end the book of Isaiah witnesses to a God who cares about much more than only the chosen people Israel. There is clearly an explicit story made necessary by the particularity of history, one that centers on a particular people through whom God has chosen to work. But there is also an implicit story in the Bible that continues to insist that God acts in love for all people in every place.

God's special people are important, to be sure, but their significance rests, at least in part, on their role as a model used to demonstrate what really matters to God, to bring God's blessing to all the nations. God expects the human community to order itself justly and to live harmoniously in peace. When Judah or any nation did not live up to this expectation, divine punishment was announced. When circumstances warranted, God was prepared to redeem the wayward and give them a new beginning. That had been the experience of Isaiah's people from the earliest days.

According to Isaiah and those who followed him, however, God's concern was not limited to Judah. All the foreigners, the nations, the others, were included in the divine drama remembered and celebrated by the covenant people, the chosen. Take note: for an eighth- or sixth-century Judahite to be told by one of God's prophets that outsiders, idol worshipers, enemies, mattered to God was extraordinary. To hear that the Lord could bring them into divine service by a mere whistle was mind-boggling. To learn that the nations were included in the positive aim of God—that the peoples would come to receive the blessings of God's instruction and love—was both a revolutionary notion and no doubt profoundly disturbing for the supernationalists of the time. Though God seemed to be exclusivistic, divine action was intended for the inclusion of all.

To be sure, the redemption of the outsiders is couched in the language of covenant relationship (Isaiah 55–56). After all, that was the religious language of the day. But the amazing aspect of the message is that God in fact valued and claimed these others as well. They were not part of Israel, and had even, at times, been hostile oppressors of God's special people. Nonetheless, they heeded God's whistle when summoned and would benefit from the divine intention to redeem and restore, ultimately to bring the whole creation to proper relationship with the Creator. From the perspective of those Isaiah addressed in the eighth century, the expanding reach of divine love was surprising, perhaps even shocking. Two centuries later, in the midst of the exile and shortly thereafter, the message was still novel and difficult to embrace. From God's vantage point there were no insiders and outsiders, only humans in need of direction and love. What is the message these words convey today amid the messy diversity of our day?

Yes, times were tough in '35, and they remained difficult throughout the lifetime of Isaiah son of Amoz. Indeed, the underlying causes of Judah's malaise, a basic disregard for God's ways, continued uncorrected for more than a century after Isaiah's time. It took a disaster in the national life to bring the people to a place of repentance and a readiness to begin again to move along God's path. Nonetheless, in the midst of all the uncertainties the prophet Isaiah, and those who followed in his steps, carefully and persistently challenged the people of Judah to recognize and celebrate the wonder and wideness of their Creator's love. God, the Holy One, cared enough to punish a wayward people, namely Judah, and thereby to risk losing their allegiance and love. Furthermore, all the nations belonged to God and none was to be left behind. The prophets reminded the people repeatedly that God was attentive and nearby, indeed only a whistle or prayer away. Faithful trust in God, expectant waiting on God, was the avenue to follow to find the security so desperately desired. Times were tough, but divine love was more than sufficient to meet the need.

Chapter Seven

Who Is My Neighbor?

Watching the evening news on TV these days, if nothing else, is an exercise in both sociology and geography. The reports come from places as distant in miles as they are different in culture: Manama, Bahrain; Crawford, Texas; Kabul, Afghanistan; Singapore; Malaysia; Zanzibar; Lima (Ohio or Peru?); and so on. Sometimes the report offers helpful information about the geographical/sociological setting. More often the report assumes that the viewer has the knowledge necessary to place the report into its proper context. But such an assumption is wrong in all too many instances.

For many Americans such knowledge is totally lacking or at best confused. Incredible as it may seem, the results of a survey reported by the National Geographic Society (November 20, 2002) revealed that among 18-to-24-year-old Americans, 87 percent could not locate Iraq on a world map, 58 percent could not find Japan, 65 percent did not know where France was, 69 percent were at a loss to locate the United Kingdom, for 29 percent the location of the Pacific Ocean was unknown, and believe it or not, 11 percent could not even find the United States on the world map. Of course, the culture of each of those many places from which the news comes is also largely a mystery. For all too many people, if they watch the news at all, the vast differences flashed on the tube become a blur, and the operative interpretive lens becomes merely "us versus them."

Whether it is comfortable or desirable, the world is shrinking. Peoples across the globe are much closer to one another now than they were even fifty years ago. Communication between locations thousands of miles apart has become almost instantaneous. A bombing in Colombia, a kidnapping in the Philippines, a heart transplant in Kentucky, each can be experienced almost immediately in numerous places around the world. For some people this news overload creates such anxiety that they quit watching TV and reading the paper. But this does not change the reality they resist. What happens in Gaza does affect (eventually, in some way) what happens in Minneapolis. The neighborhood is decidedly smaller. But there are more and more neighbors who are total strangers. How are we to relate with one another? Who is my neighbor, after all?

That question, of course, is hardly new. Some two thousand years ago an itinerant teacher named Jesus was questioned on this very matter. Jesus grew up in Nazareth, a village in Galilee, now located in modern Israel. A short three miles away was the much larger city of Sepphoris, which served as the regional capital and commercial center of the area. Sepphoris was not yet the major Roman city it became in the decades after the time of Jesus, but it was still much more cosmopolitan than Nazareth.

It is quite likely that Jesus visited Sepphoris on marketing and even recreational excursions. Perhaps he worked there in his youth as a carpenter with his father, since a number of construction projects were underway in those years. Travelers visiting Sepphoris came and went in large numbers and represented many different nationalities. It is quite likely that Jesus encountered some of these strangers, or at least heard tales about them. Even Samaritans, generally held in low esteem by Judeans and Galileans, visited Sepphoris.

But back to the question about neighbors. Jesus' teaching on this matter, according to the Gospel of Luke (Luke 10:25–37), was as engaging as it was provocative. It came about in this way. Jesus was traveling about teaching here and there. A rival Torah teacher, or "lawyer," tried to show Jesus up by quizzing him on Jewish tradition, namely the Torah or law of Moses. "What," the lawyer asked, "must I do to inherit eternal life?" Jesus replied asking the lawyer what Scripture taught. The man answered by quoting from Deuteronomy 6:5 and Leviticus 19:18: "You shall love the Lord your God with all your heart, and with all your soul, and with all your strength, and with all your mind; and your neighbor as yourself." Jesus acknowledged that the lawyer had answered the question appropriately, but then, as Luke puts it, "wanting to justify himself, the lawyer asked Jesus, 'And who is my neighbor?'"

At this point Jesus told a story. A man was traveling from Jerusalem to Jericho. This road was steep and rugged and a favorite place for robbers to set ambushes, but it was the main way to get from the hill country surrounding Jerusalem to Galilee in the north and beyond. The trade route in the Jordan Valley followed the Jordan River to the north and then connected with roads that led to the King's Highway (on the other side of the river), which in turn led to Mesopotamia. The Jordan Valley provided the main route north from Jerusalem, at least if one did not want to pass through the region of Samaria.

Samaria was a province located between Judea and Galilee. The area had, many centuries earlier, constituted a major portion of the northern kingdom called Israel. Israel had separated from Judah in 922 BCE to become an independent nation. Assyria destroyed Israel in 722 BCE. Many of the leading citizens and artisans were deported by the Assyrians. Foreigners were brought in by the Assyrians and transplanted in and around Israel's former capital city, Samaria.

Across the years some of these foreigners intermarried with Israelites who had been left behind after the 722 BCE deportation. There emerged a group of people who thought of themselves as followers of the Torah, though they had a slightly different version of the text from that canonized by a later generation of Jews. But these Samaritans did not acknowledge the priesthood of Jerusalem as the supreme religious authority, nor did they feel compelled to offer sacrifice only in Jerusalem. In fact, they had their own temple located on the summit of Mount Gerizim, which rose above the site of ancient Shechem (modern Nablus, a major city in the West Bank), famous as the place Abraham and Sarah first stopped on their journey through the land of Canaan.

In the eyes of the Judeans (often the term is translated as "Jews" but that is not really accurate until the second century CE) the Samaritans were a mongrel race of idolaters with whom no Judean should have any dealings. That is why the dangerous road down into the Jordan Valley was followed, though it would have been far more direct to follow the well-established road due north from Jerusalem passing through Samaria and down through the Esdraelon Plain and through the Valley of Jezreel to reach the trade route leading to Mesopotamia. Such is the irrational stranglehold that prejudice posing as religion often exercises.

All of this is pertinent to understanding the power of Jesus' response to the question, "And who is my neighbor?" Jesus told a story about a traveler, presumably a Judean, following the road from Jerusalem to Jericho who was attacked and left for dead by bandits. Several people passed by, including a priest (presumably from the Temple in Jerusalem) and a Levite (another of the personnel associated with the Jerusalem religious establishment centered at the Temple). Neither of these people stopped to help.

Though Jesus did not make any effort in his story to explain the behavior of the priest and Levite, it would be wrong to assume that they were just bad people who did not care that someone had been injured or even murdered. More likely, they would have been good people who had to make a decision. The guy by the roadside no doubt looked to be in pretty bad shape. If the traveler was already dead, or if he died while they were attending him, then they would have become unclean, contaminated, because they had touched a dead body. This would have made it necessary for them to seek ritual cleansing before they could resume their responsibilities. And, they probably reasoned, someone else will come by soon enough. Thus they passed by.

Of course, in Jesus' story someone indeed came by and stopped to help: a Samaritan, of all people! A Samaritan, a member of a hated and denigrated people. How could he be the hero of Jesus' story? But he was. This unnamed Samaritan cared for the injured man and rescued him from possible death. He did not expect any reward. He merely did what was needed to deal with a human catastrophe. He acted out of human compassion for someone obviously in need.

After Jesus completed the story, he returned to the original question about "neighbor" posed by the lawyer, the religious teacher. "Which of these three [the priest, the Levite, the Samaritan], do you think," Jesus asked the lawyer, "was a neighbor to the man who fell into the hands of the robbers?" The answer was really a no-brainer. From the standpoint of the wounded man, and indeed from the vantage of anyone who considered the situation, clearly the Samaritan had acted as neighbor. The lawyer admitted the obvious. Then the provocative side of Jesus' response was delivered. Jesus told him to go on his way and to act in the same manner as the Samaritan. The Samaritan in his neighborly care for the other dramatically demonstrated fulfillment of the instruction in the Torah, to love God and to love one's neighbor as oneself.

The story crafted by Jesus not only reveals what he considered to be an appropriate response to God's admonition to live a life characterized by neighborly love. It also suggests that Jesus believed that God loved in the same manner. Certainly a reading of the Old Testament, or the First Testament, as some Christians prefer to call it, or simply the Bible so far as Jews are concerned, will readily attest this insight. God's love is perceived as reaching out in an ever more inclusive circle as the biblical story unfolds. The number of people touched by God's incredible love grows and grows and grows. Each one becomes a possible agent of neighborly love.

Two particular accounts about people who lived long before Jesus illustrate the character of neighborly love. One is the story of a Moabite woman who, according to tradition, was the great-grandmother of King David, into whose line Jesus of Nazareth was born (Ruth 4:21–22; Matthew 1:5). The narrative context is the time of the judges, somewhere around 1060 BCE. The book was written, however, somewhat later (950 to 700 BCE or even as late as the exilic or postexilic periods, 550 to 450 BCE). There is considerable scholarly debate on this matter. The date of writing is certainly important for determining the intention of the author, and the scholarship should not be ignored, but the dating of the book does not affect its value as an illustration of neighborly care.

The story begins in Moab, a nation located on the east side of the Dead Sea, a small part of what is now the country of Jordan. According to biblical tradition the Moabites were descended from an incestuous union between Lot, Abraham's nephew, and Lot's oldest daughter, a rather ignoble beginning to say the least (Genesis 19:30–38). (If a Moabite version of the relationship existed, it might read differently.) A man named Elimelech with his wife, Naomi, and their two sons, Mahlon and Chilion, moved from Bethlehem in Judah, located about five miles south of Jerusalem, to Moab to escape a severe famine. In the course of time Elimelech died. Naomi and her sons stayed in Moab, and the boys each married a Moabite woman, the one Orpah and the other Ruth. After about ten years, disaster struck the family. Mahlon and Chilion died. Naomi and her daughters-in-law, Orpah and Ruth, were now all widows, left with no male to care for or defend them. In that day and time, that situation was very hazardous.

In light of her desperate situation Naomi decided to return to her family in Bethlehem across the Jordan in the hill country of Judah. In accord with custom, Naomi released her widowed daughters-in-law, Orpah and Ruth, from any obligation to her. She urged them to return to their own Moabite families. Naomi loved Orpah and Ruth, and they cared for her. But as they were both young enough to remarry and to have children, it was clearly in their best interests to leave Naomi and return to their homes. Their families might well be able to arrange second marriages for them, and under the circumstances there was no shame in that. Moreover, Naomi was not at all certain how Moabite women might be received back in Bethlehem, even if they were related to her.

With some reluctance Orpah yielded to Naomi's urging and returned to her mother's house. But Ruth would not turn away. Ruth's response to Naomi is one of the most eloquent passages in the Bible:

> Do not press me to leave you
>   or to turn back from following you!
> Where you go, I will go;
>   where you lodge, I will lodge;
> your people shall be my people,
>   and your God my God.
> Where you die, I will die—
>   there will I be buried.
> May the LORD do thus and so to me,
>   and more as well,
> if even death parts me from you!
>   Ruth 1:16–17

As the story turned out, Naomi did allow Ruth to accompany her back to Bethlehem, where Ruth eventually wed Boaz, a well-to-do relative of Naomi. The story ends on that happy note and with acknowledgment that King David himself had descended from this Bethlehemite family.

What is worth pondering in light of the question about neighbors is the way Ruth is portrayed. She was a foreigner, a Moabitess, as already noted. After she was widowed, she had no legal obligation to Naomi at all. Her normal response should have been like that of Orpah to go on home to her mother. But what would this have meant for Naomi? What would it have been like to travel alone through some rather difficult terrain and climb up that road that connected Jericho with Jerusalem? Hard enough for two unescorted women, but probably impossible for one alone. And what did it mean for Ruth to be willing to sever all ties with her family and heritage, to change even her religion? Ruth exemplifies strength and courage, resolve and ingenuity. Hers was a surprising demonstration of devoted loyalty, "covenant love." This is the kind of love that characterizes God.

Though Naomi was more than a neighbor to Ruth, Ruth's love for Naomi was the kind of love that was pleasing to God. Jesus spoke of this love as a reaching out to someone in need even though to help was costly and risky and might well go unappreciated. After all, what good could possibly come from a Samaritan? Ruth's love is of the same order. Her love was costly and risky and might well have been misunderstood by Naomi and Naomi's relatives in Bethlehem. "What is that Moabite woman really up to? Is she trying to take advantage of Naomi? What does she expect from Naomi in return for having brought her home? Such love must have some strings attached!" But Ruth's love had no strings attached. She was truly neighbor to Naomi at a most critical moment and in a most profound way. That she was a foreigner makes the story all the more remarkable. God's love reaches well beyond the expected boundaries and is embraced and enacted by the most unlikely of people. Once again the explicit narrative is augmented in an important way by the implicit aim of God's love.

"Unlikely people" is again at the core of the second of the ancient stories reflecting the character of divine love. In an unexpected way, it too offers some idea of what God expects with the instruction that the love of neighbor is every bit as important as love for God. The story has to do with an unwilling prophet sent to preach to the worst of his people's enemies with the aim of bringing them to repentance and divine forgiveness. The prophet was Jonah, and the hated Assyrians were his audience. The narrative setting for the story seems to have been mid-ninth century BCE, but it was probably written many years later, after Assyria was no longer a world power. In the story Assyria is a symbol for evil and rebellion against God, much like Rome will become in later Jewish and Christian literature.

The story is relatively brief and to the point. It is most likely historical fiction, weaving an instructional tale around an otherwise quite obscure prophet named Jonah, who lived somewhere between 786 and 746 BCE in the northern kingdom Israel (Jonah 1:1; 2 Kings 14:25). Jonah was instructed to go to Nineveh, the capital of Assyria, to announce God's impending punishment on them for their wickedness. Jonah did not want to go to Nineveh (for reasons that will become apparent at the end of the story). So he set sail in the opposite direction trying to escape his assignment.

God sent a great storm in order to halt Jonah's flight. Perhaps one of the best-known episodes in the Bible involves Jonah's taxi ride in the belly of a "large fish" (some insist "whale") after he was thrown overboard (Jonah 1:17–2:10). Much debate has centered on whether such a "belly ride" is possible or not. For the story, the historicity issue is absolutely unimportant. The narrative function of the critter that swallows Jonah is to demonstrate God's ability and willingness to save the rebellious prophet and to ensure that Jonah does not avoid his divinely appointed task Jonah's effort at flight was thwarted.

Then, the Bible reports, God addressed the reluctant messenger a second time, instructing him once again to go to Nineveh (Jonah 3:1). Jonah's message was straightforward: "Forty days more, and Nineveh shall be overthrown" (3:4). In terms of historicity, questions again arise. How could a prophet from Israel make it to the capital of Assyria and walk about freely and without challenge? What does it mean to say the city was "three days' walk across" when the archaeological evidence reveals a large city, but not one that under usual circumstances would take three days to traverse (Jonah 3:3)?

Of course, such questions are irrelevant for the point of the story. What the narrator wants to underscore is that Jonah was delivering God's word of impending punishment to the hated Assyrians right in the center of that detested empire. No doubt Jonah took some pleasure in announcing the coming disaster. Israel's enemies deserved divine condemnation. In forty days Assyria would be overthrown! This was good news for all those who had been afflicted and oppressed by the Assyrians, and there were many.

But the punishment did not come. Why? Because when the populace of Nineveh heard Jonah's message, they repented. When the (unnamed) king heard what was going on, he too joined in fasting and repentance in the hope that God's punishment might be averted (Jonah 3:5–9). At this point in the story, we learn why Jonah had been so reluctant to go to Nineveh in the first place. Jonah knew that the Lord "was a gracious God and merciful, slow to anger, and abounding in steadfast love, and ready to relent from punishing" (4:2). Jonah did not want God to forgive the hated Assyrians. Thus Jonah did not want to go to Nineveh. He did not want to become the means of God's saving forgiveness that he knew would come if the Assyrians repented. The whole city responded to Jonah's "preaching," according to the story, and Jonah became despondent (4:3–5). Jonah did not love the Assyrians, though they were his neighbors, and he did not want God to love them either. But God did, and that was the point of the whole story (4:10–11).

The historical and literary contexts of each of these narratives about foreigners have at least two things in common. They were each addressed to insiders who assumed God's love had been extended to them but not to others outside the covenants of Moses and David. What was the message? The lawyer was told to model his behavior after that of a detested Samaritan if he wanted truly to live by God's commands. Those insiders who heard the story of Ruth's incredible devotion to Naomi were forced to consider how an outsider, a Moabitess of all people, had become an integral part of God's story. Jonah's account made dramatically clear that insider disdain, even hate, for outsiders, even if they were enemies who had done terrible things to Israel, could not subvert or circumscribe God's love.

The second way each of these passages is related rests in what is disclosed about the character of God's love of others. The Samaritan in Jesus' story showed what love of neighbor was all about. Indirectly, Jesus' story disclosed that God was concerned for those in great need and provided help, often in the most unlikely of ways. Ruth's devotion to Naomi demonstrated on a human level what God's love, God's devoted loyalty to Israel and to humankind, was all about. Devoted loyalty was not flighty sentimentality. God's love was reliable, had staying power and constancy. Ruth the Moabitess provided a living example of what God's love involved. Jonah in turn showed just how far God was prepared to go by extending divine love, even to, especially to, those least deserving. Jesus, perhaps informed by the very example of God, instructed his followers to love even their enemies. As Matthew reports it: "But I [Jesus] say to you, Love your enemies and pray for those who persecute you, so that you may be children of your Father in heaven; for he makes his sun rise on the evil and on the good, and sends rain on the righteous and on the unrighteous" (Matthew 5:44–45).

For all who long to live together peaceably and respectfully, the answer to the question "Who is my neighbor?" has special importance. It is clear that many in the world define "neighbor" in very narrow ways, just as in biblical times. It is equally clear that knowing who is my neighbor and loving my neighbor are not necessarily the same. The Bible repeatedly stresses that all people live in God's neighborhood and are thus obligated to act neighborly. Jesus turned the issue away from "Who is my neighbor?" to "Who was a neighbor to the man who fell into the hands of the robbers?" (Luke 10:29, 36).

Each person who loves God, and who, in turn, wants to love in the same way that the Bible portrays God loving, needs to have a loving intention. The circle of God's love is wide. Each needs to ask daily, How can I be neighbor today to the woman next door, to the man across the street, to my family, to my colleagues at work? Indeed, how can I be neighbor even to people I don't know personally but whose lives intersect with mine because of the economic or political realities of the world today? What do I need to learn about others? How can I let others learn about me?

There is no easy answer to these questions, no single solution.

Nonetheless, learning about our neighbors and acting as neighbor toward others is of fundamental importance for our times. At the least, it means caring about others and concretely reaching out to help those around us and those in other lands who are hurting, even those who meet us as an enemy.

Chapter Eight

Light Is Light, Whoever Holds the Candle

*B*enjamin Franklin is renowned for many things, not the least being his proverbs or wise sayings. Some are very well known; some are quite obscure; most are certainly insightful. Here are just a few. "Early to bed, early to rise, makes a man healthy, wealthy, and wise." "To err is human, to repent divine, to persist devilish." "Poverty wants some things, luxury many things, avarice all things." "Eat to live, and not live to eat." "Beware of the young doctor and the old barber." "He that lies down with dogs shall rise up with fleas." "A full belly makes a dull brain." (As found at www.pocanticohills.org/franklin/sayings.htm.)

One does not have to look far for many more wise sayings and proverbs, fashioned in the Benjamin Franklin mode. These pieces of wisdom are believable because they ring true to human experience. For example, from Japanese Buddhist sources: "Better to shave the heart than to shave the head"; "All lust is grief"; and "The flower goes back to its root" (as found at www.sacred-texts.com/shi/igj/igj12.htm). From the great Chinese teacher Confucius: "Guide the people by law, subdue them by punishment; they may shun crime, but will be void of shame. Guide them by example, subdue them by courtesy; they will learn shame, and come to be good." "Study without thought is vain; thought without study is dangerous." In response to an inquiry about the whole of human duty, Confucius replied, some five hundred years before the time of Jesus, "Fellow-feeling, perhaps. Do not do unto others, what thou wouldst not they should do unto thee" ("Confucius" II, 3, 15; and XV, 23).

It is not uncommon to hear someone comment, "As the Bible says, 'A penny saved is a penny earned.'" Of course, the famous saying belongs to Benjamin Franklin, not the Bible. But it is remembered as if it were "biblical" because there is clearly truth to what he said. Of course, the saying probably needs to be altered today to "A hundred saved is a hundred earned," but the frugality that Franklin was advocating is still important to consider. His observation may not always be pertinent to a situation, but it often is, and it matters not whether it is biblical. When there is darkness, light from any source is of help. Useful observations about how best to live can come from many different places. A wise person will learn truth from whatever source it may come. To be sure, everything that may look at first to be true may not always prove to be so. But, as Franklin put it, "When the well's dry, we know the worth of water." Light is light; truth is truth.

Because God created human beings as rational creatures able to learn from their experiences, what is known as "wisdom literature" came into being. The proverbs already mentioned represent only a fraction of the sayings and instruction of the "wise" teachers that can be found in cultures all around the world dating from as early as the third millennium BCE. Besides proverbs, there are parables, riddles, numerical sayings, admonitions, similitudes, and a number of other genres (types of literature) and rhetorical devices employed in the teaching of wisdom. Elders passed on what they had learned about life to children, in the home and in the wider activities of the family. Teachers offered instruction on how best to get along within the realities of business circles and political structures. The bottom line for this kind of truth is human experience, and it is powerful.

The test of wisdom is not whether an observation is always true but, rather, whether it is true in at least some circumstances. To save a penny may not always be wise, but, often, depending upon circumstances, it may be the most prudent action to take. The truths that are found in the world's wisdom writings are distilled from life, from what works, from what is useful for getting along in at least some, if not all, of the circumstances of real life.

The wisdom traditions are full of observations about the natural world as well. The perseverance of an ant offered an insight useful for shaping human behavior and so it was noted (Proverbs 6:6). Recognizing the reliability of the seasons and the inevitability of death helped wisdom teachers instill in their students a proper respect for the mysteries of creation and for existence (Ecclesiastes 1:4–11). Cataloging the flora and fauna and the movements of the stars served to emphasize the vastness and complexity of a world in which humans, though important, were nonetheless but a part (1 Kings 4:32–33; Sirach 42:15–43:33).

In the Bible there are numerous wisdom contributions. From the prophet Isaiah of Jerusalem (Isaiah 28:23–29) to Jesus of Nazareth (Matthew 5:13–16; 7:6; 13:1–9), examples of wisdom teaching can be found. Some psalms reflect wisdom style and motifs (for instance, Psalms 1, 37, 49, 73). The magi who visited Jesus at his birth were wise men, possibly astrologers (Matthew 2:1–12). Then there are the First Testament books of Proverbs, Job, Ecclesiastes (and in Orthodox and Roman Catholic Bibles, the Wisdom of Solomon and the Wisdom of Jesus the Son of Sirach), as well as the Second Testament book of James, that are written in the style of wisdom and preserve some of the important teachings and reflections of the wise.

The wisdom writings in the Bible were not written in a vacuum. The tradition of the visit of the queen of Sheba reflects the interchange that took place between countries and cultures. The queen came to test Solomon with hard questions in the style of the wisdom teachers. After an extended discussion, the queen affirmed Solomon's "wisdom and prosperity" (1 Kings 10:7). Solomon became the patron of the wisdom tradition with the books of Proverbs and Ecclesiastes (as well as the Wisdom of Solomon) attributed to him. While there is much material that could have come from the hand of Israel's famous king, there is also much in each of these books that seems to derive from a much later time than that of Solomon.

Furthermore, some material in Proverbs, namely the "teaching of the wise" (Proverbs 22:17–24:22), closely parallels an Egyptian writing known as the Instruction of Amenemope (Pritchard 1969, 421–24). And Ecclesiastes has both an Egyptian parallel (A Song of the Harper [Pritchard 1969, 467]) and a Babylonian counterpart (A Dialogue about Human Misery [Pritchard 1969, 438–40]). How directly these various writings are related to one another is debated, but the point is that wisdom in Israel was part of a much wider tradition of observation and reflection. Ancient folk searched for understanding and shared, debated, and recorded various insights or truths that resonated with their experience of life. Neither nationality nor religion guaranteed or disqualified what was recognized as "wisdom." Experience was the adjudicator.

Probably the most famous of the biblical wisdom writings is the book of Job. Various aspects of the book's content have prompted a wide variety of modern reactions. From poet Robert Frost's *A Masque of Reason* (1945) to C. G. Jung's psychoanalytic *Answer to Job* (1952) to Archibald MacLeish's Pulitzer Prize winning play *JB: A Play in Verse* (1956) to Elie Wiesel's stunning drama *The Trial of God: A Play in Three Acts* (1977) to Gustavo Gutiérrez's probing *On Job: God-Talk and the Suffering of the Innocent* (1987), reflections inspired by Job have intrigued and challenged contemporary audiences.

Not much is known about the biblical Job apart from the book in which he is the hero, not the author. The opening verse identifies him as "a man in the land of Uz" (Job 1:1). The location of Uz is disputed, but most scholars situate it in either ancient Edomite or Aramean territory, east of the deep Jordan Valley rift that separates the modern countries of Jordan and Israel. The author of the book of Job, writing probably in the sixth century BCE, cast Job, a non-Israelite, "a man in the land of Uz," in the leading role. The names of Job's three friends indicate that they too were from non-Israelite areas: Eliphaz the Temanite, Bildad the Shuhite, and Zophar the Naamathite (2:11). The circle of God's loving concern was obviously envisioned as much wider than many today often assume.

In the biblical book of Ezekiel there is a brief reference to a Job who is associated with Noah and Danel (Ezekiel 14:14, 20). Noah was the righteous non-Israelite or pre-Israelite whose story we have already visited. Ezekiel's Danel was probably the legendary Canaanite king, known for his wisdom (28:3) and righteousness, whose story is found in a writing known as the Aqhat Epic, discovered in 1930–1931 CE when a huge library of texts was unearthed at Ras Shamra (ancient Ugarit), located on the northern coast of modern Syria. This Danel is not to be confused with the Daniel of the biblical book of Daniel, though that Daniel is also pictured as a wise and virtuous man. For the writer of Job it was important to choose a hero renowned for his wisdom, one who stood tall even in the company of ancient worthies like Noah and Danel.

The only other biblical mention of Job is found in the book of James, another book that displays many marks of wisdom. James 5:7–11 admonishes the faithful to "persevere." Sometimes the Greek text of James is translated "be patient," but that is not a strong enough translation and is somewhat misleading. The point James emphasized was "endurance," "steadfastness." Nonetheless, because of some translations of James 5:11, many people today think of Job as an exemplar of "patience."

No doubt the author of James was reflecting on the prose story found in Job 1–2 and 42:7–17, where the man in Uz does indeed endure a great deal of personal suffering, including the loss of all his children and his material goods. But the bulk of the book of Job (chapters 3–41), written in poetry rather than prose, does not portray a patient man at all. Job may have endured a great deal, but patient he was not. Rather, Job is seen as one who vigorously and directly challenged both his friends and even God in his effort to make sense of his experience. That is exactly the way a wisdom writer goes at things.

The long poetic sections of Job are arranged as a dialogue—actually more a debate—between Job and his three friends Eliphaz, Bildad, and Zophar. At the end God also enters the scene and engages in direct discourse with Job. The subject of this long poetic debate is whether Job's suffering is justified. Has he done something for which he deserves to be punished? The friends maintained the truth of a wisdom teaching found in Proverbs, and elsewhere in the Bible, that human suffering was divine retribution for human wrongdoing of some form or other. The sufferer may not know that a sin has been committed, but suffering is in itself the evidence that sin has occurred and one must repent for wellness to return, for suffering to cease. Job insisted that he had done nothing that could possibly warrant the disasters that had happened to him. Indeed, Job argued, if what he experienced was divine punishment, then God was unjust.

"Theodicy" is the attempt to vindicate God from the charge of being unjust or from responsibility for evil. The obvious inequities and disasters that mar human life give rise to such charges. Such experiences cause some people to question seriously God's goodness. Others are led to deny the very existence of God. Simply put, how could a good God allow or, heaven forbid, cause evil things to happen? Such is the main concern of theodicy.

Part of the intent of Job's author was to provide a clear demonstration that the idea of retribution had limitations. There were probably times when a disaster or an illness was the result of wrongdoing, but that was not always true. The author presented a man declared upright and without sin four times in the prose section of the book, by God no less, who nonetheless suffered the pain of catastrophe (Job 1:8, 22; 2:10; 42:8). So far as the author of Job was concerned, Job's suffering could not rightly be interpreted as resulting from divine punishment. Job's situation might not be explained, but the author made clear that it need not be only endured in silence either. Authentic relationship with God required Job to speak out in protest, and to expect God to respond. This is one form of theodicy. Such is the stuff of one type of wisdom reflection, and it has a long tradition among wisdom teachers, ancient and modern.

Indeed, at least five hundred years before the writing of Job, a Babylonian author composed a wisdom text with striking formal parallels to the book of Job. It is called the "Babylonian Theodicy" or "A Dialogue about Human Misery" (Pritchard 1969, 438–40). It is arranged as a poetic dialogue between a sufferer and his friend. The sufferer, like Job, was in pain and turmoil. He could not understand why things had happened as they had. He felt himself an innocent victim. As one insightful, contemporary interpreter notes: "In each of his speeches, the Babylonian sufferer complains about either personal misfortune or his perception that the world itself is morally disordered, with the unworthy and the criminal prospering while the deserving and the pious languish in misery" (Newsom 1996, 331). The friend in turn repeatedly criticizes the sufferer for "something irrational, erroneous, or blasphemous" (Newsom, 330). The Babylonian Theodicy ends differently from the book of Job, but clearly some of the same issues are raised for consideration.

Those issues continue to puzzle and confuse and anger thoughtful human beings. The issue of evil in the world cannot easily be explained.

But it is worth talking about. When human experience is taken seriously as a legitimate basis for reflection about God, or about anything else that really matters in life, questions will arise. Different opinions will be voiced. Some will be more helpful than others, but if we thoughtfully wrestle with real life experience, we will find truth. Neither the Babylonian Theodicy nor the book of Job solves all the problems, but these writings do provide a place from which to discuss honestly some of the difficulties humans face, and that is one of the main goals of wisdom teachers.

The wisdom writings in the Bible assume God's existence without ever trying to prove it. Yes, there is a witness to God presented by the intricate creation of which all humans are a part. Yes, the majesty and work of God as creator are lauded at times. But what is important for the work of the wisdom teacher is the common humanity all human beings share. The Bible notes this by its affirmation that humankind was created in the "image of God" (Genesis 1:26–27). God did not first create Israelites or Moabites or Egyptians or Babylonians to say anything about Americans or Koreans or whoever. God did not first fashion Jews or Christians or Muslims or Taoists or Hindus. God created human beings. From the standpoint of wisdom, no religion or culture owns God. God is not ours, but all are God's. Thus human life and human experience are valuable and provide a window to learn about God's ways. Certainly plenty of voices in the Bible declare God's way, but life itself is an ongoing laboratory for learning what works, thereby enabling recognition of at least some aspects of the divine intention for human beings.

The importance of this rather obvious fact, however, often goes unrecognized, ignored, or denied. People frequently believe that they must prove their uniqueness in order to guard their value. Some Christians, for instance, totally ignoring the historical and literary context of Jesus' controversies with "certain Pharisees" in the New Testament, have vilified all Jews in their effort to claim the superiority of Christianity over Judaism. The worth of one neither requires nor is enhanced by proving the unworthiness of another. Wisdom begins with the assumption that all are valuable, though all are mortal, and all have possible contributions to share that will be worthwhile.

One more illustration may help to make this point. Christians, rightly, cherish and teach the words of Jesus that have come to be called the Golden Rule: "In everything do to others as you would have them do to you; for this is the law and the prophets" (Matthew 7:12; Luke 6:31). But this insight is hardly unique. Jesus drew his teaching from the traditions of his people. It is an obvious expansion of the instruction to "love your neighbor as yourself" (Leviticus 19:18). Tobit, written before the time of Jesus, said, "And what you hate, do not do to anyone" (Tobit 4:15). Sirach, also before Jesus, advised: "Judge your neighbor's feelings by your own, and in every matter be thoughtful" (Sirach 31:15). Later in the Talmud, Jewish tradition, drawing on some of the same sources known to Jesus, affirmed the same principle in these words of Hillel: "What is hateful to you, do not to your neighbor: that is the entire Torah; all the rest of it is commentary; go and learn" (*Shabbat* 31a). Even later still, the prophet Muhammad, drawing from the same well perhaps, taught: "None of you believes until he wishes for his brother what he wishes for himself" (no. 13 of "Al-Nawawi's Forty *Hadiths*"). Each version has its own distinctiveness, but they all encourage a respectful attitude toward the other. After all, common sense, or perhaps more accurately thoughtful reflection on life experience (i.e., wisdom), recognizes that things go better when people respect one another and interact with one another accordingly. While many may not shape their daily lives by this light, few will deny that things would be better if more people did.

As important as the Golden Rule is, for some, as a summary of Jesus' teaching, when it is placed in the wider context of world cultures it is recognized as one contribution among many that teach essentially the same thing. Confucius's version has already been noted above. Ancient Hindu tradition offered: "This is the sum of duty: do naught to others which if done to you would cause you pain" (*Mahabharata* 5:1517). In Jainism there is the teaching: "A man should wander about treating all creatures as he himself would be treated" (*Agamas Sutrakritanga* 1.11.33). Shintoism contributes: "Be charitable to all beings, love is the representative of God" (Ko-ji Hachiman Kasuga).

Many more could be cited, but these will suffice. Reflection upon human experience, no matter in which culture one stands, has led to some similar conclusions. These different (but alike) versions of the Golden Rule are regarded by some as divinely inspired, but if so, all the more they testify to the wideness of divine love that permeates the minds and hearts of people across the centuries all around the globe.

One of the most important teachings of wisdom is that there is great diversity in life and manifold varieties of human experience. Uniformity is neither possible nor desirable. To affirm truth and light from one source does not rule out all others. The wise observer will be necessarily eclectic, learning from all manner of people and situations. The truth of a wisdom teaching does not depend on its applicability in every circumstance but rather on the light it provides in meeting the changing circumstances one may encounter. "Be a craftsman in speech, so that thou mayest be strong, for the tongue is a sword to a man, and speech is more valorous than any fighting" (the Instruction for King Meri-Ka-Re; 2200 BCE, Egyptian wisdom writing [Pritchard 1969, 415]). "The tongue of the wise dispenses knowledge, but the mouths of fools pour out folly" (Proverbs 15:2; 900–500 BCE, biblical wisdom writing). "We have too many high sounding words, and too few actions that correspond with them" (Abigail Adams, in a letter to her husband John Adams in 1774). "Kind words can be short and easy to speak, but their echoes are truly endless" (Mother Teresa, twentieth-century CE religious leader). "Many wise words are spoken in jest; but they don't compare with the number of stupid words spoken in earnest" (Sam Levenson, twentieth-century CE humorist). Each of these sayings rings true, though they come from quite different times and totally different places. Some are self-consciously wisdom sayings; others are merely wise observations by thoughtful people. Each offers some light, if only a candle, for the journey to any who care to use it.

The wisdom traditions from around the world do not claim to unveil the mystery of the divine. Most religious traditions have other voices that seek to do that for the faithful. But wisdom moves along a different path. The aim is to help the traveler take the next step with more confidence, to share lessons learned about the pitfalls and the rocky places in the road. Human reason wrestling with the enormous variety of human experience is the common link among the sages transcending national and cultural boundaries. To be sure, what may work in a small rural village in central Asia may not be immediately applicable in urban America. Nevertheless, the light, no matter what the source, is generally visible no matter what the setting. Why? Because from wisdom's point of view, all human beings, no matter the differences of status and situation that divide, share a very deep commonality, namely the same basic condition of being finite and time-bound.

"To succeed, jump as quickly at opportunities as you do at conclusions." "Remember that time is money." "Nothing in life is certain except death and taxes." More wisdom from Ben Franklin, more light for the way, another candle. As the ancient proverb puts it, "Better to light a candle than to curse the darkness." The capacity to recognize and share wisdom is one of the gifts of divine love bestowed upon the whole human family. At one point, in Proverbs, Wisdom is presented as a woman and says, "The LORD created me at the beginning of his work, the first of his acts long ago. . . . Then I was beside him, like a master worker; and I was daily his delight, rejoicing before him always, rejoicing in his inhabited world and delighting in the human race" (Proverbs 8:22, 30–31). Wisdom is possible because God's wide, wide love has made it possible.

Chapter Nine

Guess Who's Invited to Dinner

Some years ago there was a powerful movie entitled *Guess Who's Coming to Dinner.* The drama revolved around a simple question: What happens when a beloved daughter brings home the man she has fallen hopelessly in love with (and intends to marry) in order to receive the family's blessing? A celebration, right? Wrong! Not if the daughter (played by Katharine Houghton) is white and the son-in-law-to-be (played by Sidney Poitier) is black. Not in the United States in 1967, even when the daughter's parents (played by Spencer Tracy and Katharine Hepburn) are portrayed as open, tolerant, unprejudiced, mature adults. For most people, white and black, biracial marriage was largely unthinkable at that time. The movie explored the multiple prejudices and raw tension inherent in the situation. What was the outcome? One thing, at least, was clear. Difference, whether racial, social, or religious, is often difficult to accommodate around the family table.

Mealtimes are an important social occasion, in the business world as well as for families. Somehow, sharing a meal with a business colleague or with a customer, or potential customer, often helps build a better relationship. Work is accomplished, and at the same time trust and understanding can grow. Families, and larger communities as well, find that sharing meals together strengthens the commitment to one another of those gathered at the table. Thus meals can be the symbolic measure of who truly belongs in whatever situation is considered. Who gets invited? Who is forgotten or intentionally ignored? How large is the table? How generous is the host? Who shows up?

Are they the kind of people one wants to eat with? At home, who is even included in the family becomes an issue. Mealtime is often taken for granted. After all, you have to eat. But sharing food at table with others can be highly significant and can shape one's whole perspective on life. Eating, it seems, is no laughing matter.

Jesus of Nazareth is remembered as eating with all manner of folk. Some of his table partners were respected leaders and some were not. Jesus' dining habits suggest the openness Jesus had to a wide variety of people. Others might not approve of his mealtime companions, but that seems to have been quite secondary so far as Jesus was concerned. The wideness of the love Jesus had for those with whom he lived and worked seems reflected by the vast array of different people with whom he was willing to break bread. A few stories will illustrate the point.

A rich tax collector (or publican) named Zacchaeus lived in Jericho (Luke 19:1–2). Now Jericho was a town that grew up around a luxurious oasis located at the north end of the Dead Sea watered by large natural springs that still produce some 550 million cubic meters of water per hour. Jericho had been an important market crossroads for centuries before the time of Jesus and provided a lucrative place of business for a man like Zacchaeus. Roman policy was to contract with some wealthy person, usually a foreigner to the region, to gather local taxes. Then a person native to the area was hired to do the actual tax collecting work. Zacchaeus, a Jew, was such a person.

Tax collectors as a group were generally detested by the local people, their neighbors, because of their close contact with the Gentiles (Romans and other non-Jews) and for adding their own surcharges to the bills collected. Zacchaeus no doubt was ostracized, suffering the social stigma that went with being a tax collector. Simply put, no good Jew of the time would have had any more contact than absolutely necessary with a sinner like Zacchaeus. Having dinner at Zacchaeus's house would have been out of the question.

Nonetheless, this is exactly what Jesus did, and at his own invitation. Zacchaeus was small of stature according to the story. Thus he climbed into a tree to catch a glimpse of the notorious Jesus whom he had heard was to pass by. When Jesus saw him, he stopped and told him to get down from the tree. Then, incredibly, Jesus invited himself to Zacchaeus's place. A good Jew would never spend the day at Zacchaeus's house, but that is what Jesus did (Luke 19:3–5). This turned out to be a life-changing event for Zacchaeus. He promised that his business practices and his relationships with others in his community would change for the better (19:8–10).

But what is of interest here is the reaction of the good people who witnessed this remarkable scene. In the cultural context of that day, it was an honor to have a guest come to your home, particularly someone well known like Jesus. So all the townspeople rejoiced at the honor bestowed on Zacchaeus by Jesus' visit, right? Wrong! Rather, they grumbled and said, "He [Jesus] has gone to be the guest of one who is a sinner" (Luke 19:7). They did not recognize what was really going on. They could not see that Jesus reached out to a man in need of a change of course. All they saw was a violation of religious etiquette. All they saw was a dinner table with the wrong people gathered together.

There is a similar story about another tax collector named Levi (perhaps also known as Matthew; Matthew 9:9). Levi became a follower of Jesus and then threw a big party in Jesus' honor at his house. And wouldn't you know, the invitation list included a lot of folk that "good people" considered unacceptable. Luke reports, "There was a large crowd of tax collectors and others sitting at the table with them" (Luke 5:28–29). Further, some religious leaders, Pharisees, complained about Jesus' behavior and asked Jesus' disciples, "Why do you eat and drink with tax collectors and sinners?" (5:30).

Apparently a number of people critical of those with whom Jesus associated said of Jesus: "Look, a glutton and a drunkard, a friend of tax collectors and sinners" (Luke 7:34). They did not care why Jesus went to Levi's house or the good news that Jesus brought with him (5:31–32); they simply were offended that Jesus had table fellowship with the wrong people, with the unclean, with sinners, with folks with whom "good people" just did not associate. Their criticism of Jesus' character should not be taken as necessarily true just because they voiced it, but the accusation does underscore that Jesus was perceived by a number of his contemporaries as, at the least, indiscriminate in the company he kept.

With the reputation Jesus had, it is perhaps surprising that, nonetheless, sometimes even "good people" invited Jesus home for dinner. Apparently the power of Jesus' personality and his teaching prompted people to seek Jesus' presence in order better to know him and to hear his views. One such occasion, again reported by Luke, involved a Pharisee named Simon who one day asked Jesus home for dinner (Luke 7:36). Now the Pharisees were good people, at least for the most part. They have gotten a bad rap among Christians because Jesus was remembered as often challenging them in heated conversation and with strong denunciations (Matthew 23). Jesus did strongly disagree with some of their teaching about how the faithful were to live, but taken as a whole, at least on the basis of what we know about the Pharisees from sources outside the New Testament, Jesus seems to have agreed with many of their central teachings. Devotion to God's ways, regard for others, trust in the power of God to resurrect the dead for judgment were common points between Jesus and the Pharisees. At least one zealous Pharisee became a prominent follower of Jesus, the apostle Paul (Philippians 3:5).

The meal Simon invited Jesus to share was apparently more than simply a bowl of soup in the kitchen. Jesus had a designated place at the table, and enough had been made of the affair that others in town had heard about it (Luke 7:36–37). Why Simon invited Jesus is never explained, but the occasion was remembered anyway, mainly because someone crashed the party. A "woman of the city, who was a sinner," walked right in. An uninvited harlot came in looking for Jesus, to the alarm and appalling dismay of Simon (7:37–39). She was an embarrassment of the first order. Did she sit quietly and listen to the dinner talk? Oh, no! She wept profusely out of thankful joy. She anointed Jesus' feet. And Simon? All he could think about was what kind of woman she was. The story was preserved as a clear example of the way Jesus was willing to forgive and to include people who were excluded in the society of the day. The "woman of the city" was not on Simon's guest list, but Jesus welcomed her, and, so far as he was concerned, she became the guest of honor.

Not only was Jesus a guest for dinner here and there, he also served as host at some memorable feasts. One took place, according to Luke, near the town of Bethsaida, the small fishing village that was home to the apostles Peter, Andrew, and Philip. The exact location of Bethsaida is debated, but it was somewhere along the northeastern shore of the Sea of Galilee. Jesus had gone there to get out of the public eye, but to no avail. A crowd of around five thousand found out that he was there and came looking for him. Good host that he was, Jesus "welcomed them, and spoke to them about the kingdom of God, and healed those who needed to be cured" (Luke 9:10–11). As night approached, the disciples told Jesus to send the crowd away so that they could find food and lodging. To their surprise, however, Jesus told his disciples that they were to feed the crowd. The disciples protested. Where could they find food for such a large crowd on such short notice? Nonetheless, Jesus insisted and, miraculously, the crowd was amply fed and there was even bread and fish left over (9:12–17).

One of the noteworthy aspects of this great event was the absence of any invitation list. Jesus did not ask for identity cards. He did not require a declaration of actual allegiance to him or even the intention to believe in him. He did not inquire whether the people gathered were clean or sinless, or consider any number of other criteria that might have been used. He did not try to limit the crowd for the sake of cost control. No, Jesus just blessed the food and had it distributed to the hungry. As he did so, perhaps he remembered the words of the prophet Isaiah: "Ho, everyone who thirsts, come to the waters; and you that have no money, come, buy and eat!" (Isaiah 55:1).

Jesus' attitude with regard to welcoming and including outsiders had a significant influence on the movement that formed around his name. The importance of table fellowship marked the early church. As Luke puts it in Acts, the early followers of Jesus "devoted themselves to the apostles' teaching and fellowship, to the breaking of bread and the prayers" (Acts 2:42). The phrase "breaking of bread" early on came to refer to the sacramental sharing of bread and wine in remembrance of Jesus' death and his last meal with his disciples. But the importance of a "Jesus meal" derived from the memory of Jesus' joyous participation on countless occasions when he shared food with all manner of folk.

As meals had at times been occasions for controversy and tension in Jesus' ministry, so they continued to be in the life of the early church.

Two special challenges were noted in the earliest writings of the New Testament, the letters of Paul. The first was perhaps limited to a particular congregation, though we cannot be certain. Paul did make clear that in the church at Corinth, a major Greek city of the first century CE, practices most offensive to the apostle were taking place. The issue seems to have centered on the times when the congregation gathered to observe the Lord's Supper. Before the liturgical remembrance took place, the wealthier members of the congregation were eating sumptuously and selfishly while poorer congregants were going hungry. Such behavior was inappropriate in terms of both community worship and community harmony (1 Corinthians 11:17–22). Paul understood clearly that this kind of discriminatory disregard of the rich for the poor was totally out of place in the church of Jesus Christ.

In the social context of Corinth the Christian movement was minuscule. The city was overwhelmingly pagan. It was imperative that the Christians maintained a common front and demonstrated what "new life in Christ" meant. The church was a community pointing beyond itself to the coming reign of God, a time of justice and peace for all. The Christians at Corinth had to behave themselves accordingly. So far as Paul was concerned, meals were to be a time when all were welcome and all were nourished.

Paul faced an even more difficult mealtime issue however, one that threatened the very life of the movement. The Christian movement began with the Galilean and Judean followers of Jesus of Nazareth. Jesus' followers were not called "Christian" until late in the first century CE, and initially the term was probably a term of derision. The early Christians understood themselves as Jews who followed a Jew named Jesus. Thus they maintained the commandments, observing the Sabbath, hoping in the God they believed had raised Jesus from the dead.

As the movement spread, however, non-Jews, Gentiles, were drawn in, and this is where Paul's problem began. Paul understood himself especially commissioned to preach to the Gentiles, to non-Jews, to those who were considered outsiders from a traditional Jewish perspective. Paul believed that God was fulfilling the promise made to Abraham (that all the nations would be blessed through him) by sending the good news of Jesus Christ to the Gentiles through Paul.

The problem came when Gentile Christians and Jewish Christians found themselves in the same congregation or in social situations like eating together. Some of the Jewish Christians believed that Gentiles had to become Jews before they could truly be Christians. Some Gentile Christians called "Judaizers," who had accepted Jewish tradition and practice and who thought of themselves as Jews, insisted that new Gentile converts had to do the same, to be circumcised and follow the same food laws that Jews and Jewish Christians followed. Paul was adamant that Gentiles did not need to become Jews, did not have to be circumcised or follow any other distinctly Jewish customs, before or after becoming Christians.

Paul's convictions brought him into bitter conflict with another of the early church's leaders, namely Peter (also known as Cephas), who had been one of the original disciples and an ardent supporter of Jesus. Peter had early on been challenged in a vision to take the gospel to the Gentiles. The vision itself is interesting because it involved various unclean creatures that Peter was instructed to kill and eat (Acts 10:12). Peter resisted, saying, "By no means, Lord; for I have never eaten anything that is profane or unclean" (10:14). To this God responded, "What God has made clean, you must not call profane" (10:15). What followed next was critical for the Christian movement, because Peter was directed to the home of a Roman centurion in Caesarea, a non-Jew, a Gentile, someone definitely unclean. Peter recognized God's intention. What God made clean was not to be scorned or avoided. Gentiles, too, fell within the wide circle of God's love. As a consequence of Peter's visit, Cornelius, the centurion, was received into the Christian movement, thus opening a new chapter in God's story (10:34–48).

Now after such a dramatic encounter with God, one might think that Peter would have gotten things right, and he apparently did for a while. But later, according to Paul, while Peter was visiting Paul and the church in Antioch, mealtime became a little dicey. Initially, Peter had taken his place at table with any who were there. But then "certain people came from James" (James was leader of the church in Jerusalem) and others known as "the circumcision faction" put pressure on Peter to separate himself from the "uncircumcised." Peter then apparently forgot his own experience and the deep conviction that flowed from it, namely that Gentiles and Jews were equally clean in God's eyes. As a result, Peter withdrew from the common table (Galatians 2:12). Others joined Peter, and the congregation was in turmoil.

Paul's reaction was strong. When he heard what had happened, he confronted Peter face-to-face. Paul insisted that everyone had a place at Christ's table. Gentiles did not need to be circumcised, that is, to become Jews, to be totally included in the church, and Peter knew it. Peter had witnessed God's grace extended to Cornelius. In council with other church leaders in Jerusalem, Peter had agreed with Paul and had acknowledged this very point (Acts 15). Refusing to eat with the Gentile Christians in the congregation at Antioch was an offense against them and the Lord, and Paul let Peter know it (Galatians 2:11–14). Jesus, who ate with "publicans and sinners," certainly would have no problem eating with uncircumcised Gentiles.

The controversy that surfaced at Antioch was not resolved quickly or completely. In fact, in the context of the last decades of the first century hostility increased between Christians who thought of themselves as Jews and those that did not. The percentage of Jews by birth declined as the movement spread around the Mediterranean basin. But the conflicts increased between the "Judaizers" ("the Jews," as Paul called them; namely Gentile Christians who felt it imperative to adopt Jewish customs) and other Gentile Christians, who, following Paul's lead, saw no such need. Bible passages reflecting these conflicts, when read with disregard of their original context, have led some Christians to an understanding of God's love and intention for the human family that misrepresents the original intent of the biblical writers. More will be said of this in the next chapter.

But for now, at least one more meal tradition echoes across the Bible and needs to be considered. In antiquity it was customary for kings to have great feasts on the occasion of their inaugurations or after victories on the field of battle. All were invited to come to share in the largesse of the king. People from far and wide came to celebrate the accomplishments of the king. It was rather like the festivities that surround the inauguration of a president or governor in the present time.

In the course of time, this meal came to be used as a symbol for the joy that would come at the end of history when God's reign would be established worldwide and bring a proper peace to all people. This eschatological feast, this heavenly meal, was described in Isaiah in these words: "On this mountain the LORD of hosts will make for all peoples a feast of rich food, a feast of well-aged wines, of rich food filled with marrow, of well-aged wines strained clear" (Isaiah 25:6). No fast food here. This was five-star dining.

Jesus alluded to this great feast in a parable. He was at the "house of a leader of the Pharisees" sharing the Sabbath meal (Luke 14:1). In the course of conversation another guest, reflecting on something Jesus said, made reference to the future kingdom of God (14:15). In response Jesus likened the coming of God's kingdom, the final inauguration of God's everlasting reign, to a great feast. The meal was planned. Invitations went out. Many indeed were invited. But on the day of the banquet when everything was ready, people began making excuses for not attending. One after another they declined. Hardly anyone was apparently going to come. The expected crowd, all the preparation, all the food, all the anticipation, down the tube!

The host might simply have written it all off and sent the caterer home. But no, the host would not be deprived of the anticipated celebration. A new, dramatically inclusive invitation list was drawn up. "Go out at once," he instructed, "into the streets and lanes of the town and bring in the poor, the crippled, the blind, and the lame" (Luke 14:21). It is important to note that in the context of Jesus' time, all those on the new invitation list were considered, at the least, as unworthy. They were not proper guests for a fancy dinner party. In fact, the crippled, the blind, and the lame were not even allowed to enter the Temple because they were considered unclean. When it became clear that there were still unfilled places at the table, even more invitations were extended to include those beyond the city limits, those found along "the roads and lanes" (14:23). The king wanted to have a party, and the guest list was adjusted to guarantee a crowd. There was plenty of room, plenty of food, plenty of everything needed to celebrate God's reign.

Jesus did not interpret the parable of the great banquet, but some of the meaning is transparent. At God's table there is plenty of room.

In the context of Luke, the message includes the implied exhortation to all to accept the invitation when it comes. Join in the celebration. This is certainly in keeping with the other meal traditions that have been considered. No mere mortal can determine who is coming to dinner. But God has made clear in the Bible that divine love is wide and all-embracing. The invitation list includes many more than can ever be counted or perhaps even imagined. God is the host, and there is a place at the table for people of every kind, even including people like us.

Chapter Ten

God's Way Made Particular

There is perhaps no single verse in the New Testament better known than John 14:6:

> Jesus said to him [Thomas], "I am the way, and the truth, and the life. No one comes to the Father except through me."

Likewise there is probably no single verse that has been more misunderstood and misused. Rather than being recognized as an invitation into a close relationship of discipleship with Jesus, the verse has been used all too often to browbeat the unsaved. Too many times arrogant assertions of religious superiority have displaced the loving Lord whose way is at issue. How did this ever happen? How did the all-embracing love of God made particular in Jesus of Nazareth come to be interpreted as the exclusive possession of only a few? Where is the truth or the life in such an understanding of Jesus' way?

As has been urged repeatedly, it is imperative to pay close attention to the context of any written or spoken word. That is especially the case with the Gospel of John and the special verse under consideration. What is the historical setting, the political and religious background for these words in this Gospel? What did everyone who lived when the Gospel was written consider self-evident, what was common knowledge that modern readers may not know or recognize? What is the literary context of this particular verse, John 14:6, within the Gospel of John itself? These questions may sound too academic, but much confusion and misunderstanding has developed because too many have ignored and even denied the context of these words for too long. Indeed, the words have been taken out of context and used in ways totally inappropriate and invalid in light of their original intent. So what is the context?

In 70 CE a catastrophe occurred in Palestine. The Temple of Herod, built on the site of Solomon's Temple, was utterly destroyed by Roman troops at the order of Emperor Vespasian. The wood in the structure was burned. Every stone in the building's walls was knocked down. Those who tried to resist were slaughtered. For the populace of Jerusalem and Judea this was a cataclysmic event. The first-century Jewish historian Josephus described the scene in this way:

> While the holy house [the Temple] was on fire, everything was plundered that came to hand, and ten thousand of those that were caught were slain; nor was there a commiseration of any age, or any reverence of gravity; but children, and old men, and profane persons, and priests, were all slain in the same manner; so that this war went round all sorts of men, and brought them to destruction, and as well those that made supplication for their lives, as those that defended themselves by fighting. . . . Nor can one imagine anything either greater or more terrible than this noise; for there was at once a shout of the Roman legions, who were marching all together, and a sad clamor of the seditious, who were now surrounded with fire and sword. (Josephus, *Jewish Wars* 6.5.1)

The world did not look the same after the smoke and dust cleared. Those who did survive were expelled from the destroyed city. In every respect, for both the Jews and Christians of Jerusalem and Palestine, this was a "9/11" event.

Jesus' ministry took place around 30–33 CE. In the years following the ministry of Jesus, but before 70 CE, the Jews in Palestine were widely diverse. There were a number of parties reflecting different understandings of what was involved in following God's way, of what it meant to live in accordance with the way revealed in the Torah (Law) and the Prophets. Despite clear disagreements and varieties of interpretations, all the members of these various parties were Jews. There was no "orthodox" position that determined who was or was not a Jew, that ruled some out and others in. Conflicting positions could and did compete. Nonetheless, all Jews were related by the fact of a common history, by revered religious traditions, and because they were a definite minority in the political and religious world of the Roman Empire.

The Essenes withdrew from the world and created a separate, monastic-like community located at Qumran along the northwestern edge of the Dead Sea. The Sadducees were associated with the priesthood in Jerusalem and had made political and religious accommodation with the Hellenistic authorities and then the Roman governors placed over them by the imperial power, first of Athens and then Rome. The Pharisees (mostly teachers or interpreters of the Torah) exerted a modernizing influence as they offered new interpretations of the tradition intended to make living in God's way more possible in the changed circumstances of the first century CE. There were also various radical groups, militants or nationalists, known as Zealots, and apocalyptic resisters who rejected the rule of all foreign powers and were ready and willing to join armed rebellion against the oppressors or, at the least, to participate to the death in passive resistance.

And there were the Christians. As already mentioned, these Jews were not called "Christians" until near the end of the first century CE. They were simply Jews who recognized in Jesus of Nazareth the distinctive work of the gracious God celebrated in the traditions of the Jews, the God whom Jesus called "Abba" (Father). At the outset of the Christian movement the disciples, and most other followers of Jesus the Jew, were themselves Jews. This must not be forgotten. Not until twenty-five or thirty years after Jesus' crucifixion and resurrection did any significant number of non-Jews (Gentiles) begin to join the movement, and most of those persons lived outside Palestine in Asia Minor and elsewhere around the Mediterranean basin. Before 70 CE the vast majority of "Christians" in Palestine understood themselves to be Jews who had a special allegiance to Jesus and who looked to Jesus as the guarantor of their deliverance from sin and death by God's gracious love. They constituted another of the many different groups of Jews and understood themselves accordingly. Indeed, it would take at least another century, perhaps two, before Christianity would be clearly separated and distinguished from Judaism.

After 70 CE, however, things Jewish in Palestine began to change in some dramatic ways. As already noted, Jews were forcibly expelled from Jerusalem. Qumran, the principal site of the Essenes, was destroyed by the Roman legions in 68 CE, thus rendering the Essenes even less a determinative voice in the post-70 reconstruction of the Jewish community. The Sadducees lost their power base with the destruction of the Jerusalem Temple. The nationalistic groups, including the apocalyptic sects, were blamed for the military disaster and lost credence with many Palestinian Jews. If there was any lingering doubt, such was dispelled when the Zealot Simon Bar Kochba, claiming to be the Messiah, led a revolt in 132–135 CE. Once again the wrath of Rome fell on Palestine. Bar Kochba was killed, Jerusalem was plowed under, and many more Jews were expelled, not only from the vicinity of Jerusalem but from greater Palestine as well.

One of the pre-70 groups of Jews survived, however, and became the establisher of what is known now as Judaism. In 69 CE, during the siege of Jerusalem, Emperor Vespasian ordered that a teacher (rabbi) of the Pharisees named Johanan ben Zakkai be allowed to leave Jerusalem and go to a town named Jabneel (also known as Jamnia or Jabne), about fifty miles west of Jerusalem at the edge of the coastal plain. There, Johanan ben Zakkai began a rabbinic/Pharisaical community that was to struggle for decades with Jewish identity.

Prior to this time there was no religion that could rightly be called "Judaism." The ancient Israelites had worshiped the God of the covenant, and the traditions of the ancient forebears were obviously foundational for the Jews gathered at Jabneel. But it was they who began to define and develop Judaism, and they did so in terms of their own Pharisaical/rabbinic understanding of the tradition. They eventually determined the canon of Jewish scripture, deciding which books would be included in the Bible and which would be omitted. They also began the work of developing the Mishnah, numerous interpretations and reflections based on tradition, which stands at the base of the Talmud, which in turn is fundamental to contemporary Judaism. Some 250 rabbinic scholars left Jabneel and went to Usha near Haifa in 135 CE, after the Romans put down the revolt of Bar Kochba, to complete the development of the Mishnah.

The sacred texts, and the methods for debating and interpreting the meaning of those texts, as well as a kind of agreed upon liturgical practice (orthopraxis), were in place. From the diversity of practice that had been so evident during the time of Jesus, the party of the Pharisees had prevailed. It would not be until the fourth century of the Common Era that Judaism as a religion was clearly defined, but by the end of the second century CE Judaism was well on the way to being established. (It is important to note that many of the same things were happening during this same time period within the Christian movement, with the rich diversity of the first century giving way to the orthodoxy that largely prevailed by the end of the third century.)

In the last decades of the first century CE, the issue of Jewish self-identity turned ugly, at least in some local situations, with regard to Jews who followed Jesus' way. As the rabbinic orthopraxis being shaped at Jabneel began to become normative for Palestinian Jews, conflicts with those of different perspective began to occur. The rise of orthopraxy—one practice of the tradition that was determinative for all true members—brought a new possibility that had not existed among Jews prior to 70 CE, namely heresy or at least nonconformity. Jews who would not toe the line with regard to the rabbinic interpretation of the tradition were considered out of line. Nonconformists are inherently dangerous to have around in that they are living reminders of dissent and diversity. As Christian theology demonstrates clearly, orthodoxy and heresy go hand in hand, and usually the truth is somewhere in between.

Around 90 CE, at least according to Christian sources, a new tool to be used against heretics, and against Christians who were now associated with the heretical undesirables, appeared. Into a liturgical document known as the Eighteen Benedictions a nineteenth was placed in the twelfth slot. This added "benediction" was more malediction than blessing. It has come to be known as the Benediction Against Heretics. This set of benedictions is still found in contemporary Jewish prayerbooks, but across the centuries the sharpness of the added piece has been decidedly softened; the strong malediction voiced in the original is not even recognizable in the versions now used.

There is a text, however, that probably gives a better sense of the original. This manuscript was found in 1896 among documents recovered from the genizah (a depository for manuscripts no longer in use) of a synagogue in Cairo, Egypt. In translation the twelfth of the nineteen benedictions, the Benediction Against Heretics, reads:

> For the apostates let there be no hope and let the arrogant government be speedily uprooted in our days. Let the Nazarenes [Christians] and the Minim [heretics] be destroyed in a moment and let them be blotted out of the Book of Life and not be inscribed with the righteous. Blessed art thou, O Lord, who humblest the proud! (O'Day 1995, 658)

The appearance of this strong denunciation of those who deviated from the orthodox norm marked a new chapter in the relationship of rabbinic Jews with Christian Jews, and, for that matter, with other groups of Jews who before 70 CE had coexisted amid the great diversity of understandings that was characteristic of Judaism before the destruction of Jerusalem.

In this context the Gospel of John was written. The exact time and place of writing continues to be debated among scholars, but most consider it likely that John was written somewhere around 90 CE. Most likely, those addressed by the Gospel were Jews who were followers of Jesus. They knew the traditions of their forebears and lived as Jews were expected to live. Non-Jews living around the congregation addressed by John would probably have seen little difference between these Jews who were Christians and other Jews who were not. But Jews who used the Eighteen Benedictions (with the recently added nineteenth) had another opinion.

There is no precise information on what happened, but writings like the Gospel of John provide some clues. Tensions began to mount within synagogues between those who accepted things along the lines being fashioned by the proponents of the new orthodoxy and those who did not. Where there once had been room for differences, uniformity became the desired standard. For Jews who were Christians this meant trouble. Two times the Gospel of John records fear among Jesus' followers because of their threatened expulsion from their synagogues, and once Jesus warns of that possibility (John 9:22; 12:42; 16:2). For caring Jews, to be "put out of the synagogue" was tantamount to a death sentence. Family, friends, community celebrations marking the beginning of life, the end, and all the in-between—everything was centered in the synagogue, especially after 70 CE. In this changed circumstance, for Jews to walk in Jesus' way took on a new dimension with potentially costly, painful consequences.

The controversy among Jews about the significance of Jesus grew more and more intense as both Jews and Christians tried to define their own identities. By 150 CE there were debates going on by representatives of both groups. Whether people actually confronted one another directly or whether these events were merely on paper and shared only within the supporting community is unclear. But the rhetoric was heated and pointed. By the end of the third century CE Christians and Jews were totally separated, at least so far as the authorities were concerned. Judaism and Christianity were established as separate religions, sharing many traditions but nonetheless independent and increasingly disdainful of one another.

The Gospel of John was written as this process of self-definition was beginning for people experiencing the pain of the division that was taking place. Thus, while it includes many positive references to people who were Jews (like the disciples of Jesus, for instance), it also has numerous references that carry a tone of anger and disdain for "the Jews." The Jews that are warned against and feared, and who are at times the object of derision in the Gospel of John, are the religious authorities, those in charge in the synagogues and those who were the self-appointed (from the Gospel's perspective) guardians of the tradition. These Jews are considered enemies of Jesus and thus also of Jesus' followers.

Now with this background in mind, the verse noted at the beginning of this chapter may sound somewhat differently from sometimes presumed. These words of Jesus, in the literary context of John, were words of encouragement and assurance. In the midst of conflict and possibly mistreatment by family and friends, Jesus' followers were reminded that Jesus did offer them an authentic way of living that was in accord with God's love. Jesus was the "way" to the Father.

Jesus is not pictured in John 14 as debating abstract principles. Jesus was not trying to establish a religion. Jesus was not debating possible strategies of evangelism. Not in John 14. Rather, Jesus is pictured by the writer of John as trying to prepare his disciples for a time when he would leave them. He was assuring them that what they saw in him was the very presence of God the Father in their midst, and thus they could trust him even in the face of persecution and rejection. Jesus himself was the living and authentic way to be followed no matter what might happen. For the writer of the Gospel, the issue was not first of all doctrinal correctness. The issue was practical, a matter of maintaining loyalty within a hard-pressed congregation of Jews who had chosen to follow Jesus and who were now being expelled from their lifelong communities, their synagogues. To disregard this literary and historical context is to do violence to the words remembered and preserved.

In John, Jesus is not presented as worrying about Hindus or Muslims or Taoists or, for that matter, participants of any of the other religions of the world that we now know. Jesus as a Jew is pictured addressing an issue among Jews. Luke, in Acts 4:12, describes the Jew Peter, a disciple of Jesus, in a similar situation challenging other Jews to recognize in Jesus the saving work of God.

To take the words ascribed to Jesus and Peter out of their literary and historical contexts is to misuse them. These words are not policy statements. They reflect the rhetoric of conflict, and the struggle of a movement—very much a minority movement at the time—to account for itself and to survive. They provide encouragement and challenge for Christians to be faithful to the God whose way is exemplified in the ministry of Jesus. These words do not define how Christians should understand others but how Christians should structure their own commitments and priorities.

In John 14 Jesus announced that he was going to leave the disciples and go to a place that they knew. The text is unclear whether Jesus had Jerusalem in mind or his heavenly home. At any rate, Thomas, one of the disciples, objected that neither he nor any of the other disciples knew where Jesus was going or how to get there. Thomas wanted to know the "way." To this question Jesus responded, "I am the way, and the truth, and the life" (John 14:5–6). The point is that Jesus himself provides all a Christian needs for a full and authentic life. That "way" is intimately related to God, who is love (1 John 3:7–21), and to Jesus' strong admonition to his followers to love one another (John 15:9–17). Following Jesus, and thereby coming to the

Father, was not a matter of acknowledging doctrinal truths for his disciples but demonstrating in their individual and communal lives how Jesus and the love incarnate in him was indeed the way, the truth, and the life. When Christians were being treated as heretics, John insisted, they needed to stand firm and take comfort from their Lord, who assured them that he was truly God's gift to them and a reliable guarantor of true life.

It is worth noting, however, that there is a philosophical side to the Gospel of John. In the Gospel of John Jesus is identified with God's "Word," or in Greek, God's Logos (John 1:1–4). In Greek philosophy the Logos was more than merely a spoken word. The Logos was the divine rationality that permeated the created universe and established and maintained order. The Logos was impersonal and universal. To associate with Jesus this understanding of divine activity abroad in the created order was quite bold.

There was precedent to be sure. In the Hebrew wisdom tradition "Woman Wisdom" had earlier been portrayed as exercising the same role ascribed to the Logos in the creation of the world (Proverbs 8:22–31). Wisdom was poetically presented as a particular woman who invited all the human family to a full life guided by Wisdom and thereby in accord with God's way (8:1–21). Wisdom was the divine agent that assured order and meaning to the world. While not identical, Wisdom and/or Logos was considered a constituent of each individual that sought to direct each to the full life intended by God.

According to the Gospel of John, the bold assertion is made that the Logos, in the course of time, became flesh and was incarnated in one person. For John it is too simple to say that salvation comes through Jesus of Nazareth. For John divine deliverance is the work of the Logos who, like Wisdom, was with God in the beginning, participating in the creation of all things and bringing life and light into the world. The Logos touched every human being, not only a few. Yes, the universal was made particular, but rather than being a simple truth this is a profound mystery. In Jesus of Nazareth the Logos was "enfleshed," John declared, and God's glory was made present. God's grace and truth were fully disclosed (John 1:14–18). Thus to see Jesus the Logos was to see God (1:14). To know Jesus was and is to know

God (14:7). To declare that "no one comes to the Father except through me" in reference to Jesus, as does John 14:6, was, in the historical and literary context, to underscore the call to continued loyalty on the one hand and on the other to claim a philosophical tradition about the Logos that was widely held among first-century Jews and Greeks.

At the time when the Gospel of John was written there was no aim to eradicate Judaism. There was no intention to say that Jews, as contrasted with Christians, had no knowledge or relationship with God. The purpose was to provide a secure place for a minority of Jews, the Christians, within what was itself a minority in the Roman Empire, the rabbinic Jews, to follow its own "way," namely the way of Jesus. The purpose of John was not to establish dominance over others but rather to assure authenticity to the beleaguered. Words of comfort for "us" should not be used as words of attack or denunciation of "them." In our time we need to take this very seriously and resist efforts to exclude others by a narrow reading of the tradition. To "come to the Father," who is love, is to love as Jesus loved. That is the way, the truth, and the life.

One of the wonderful, but problematic, features of the biblical story is that God insists on meeting humankind in very particular moments and ways. God is certainly not limited to the particular persons or to the events recounted in the biblical story, nor is God the sum total of all these accounts. God cannot be abstracted from the various witnesses either and made into a set of principles or truths. In each story a glimpse of God is to be had. In the person of Jesus, God is to be met—but always in particular places, in particular times, in particular circumstances. There are an ample number of particular stories to meet the needs of those seeking the way, but not by generalizing the particulars into some unspecific guide or absolute rule. Rather, each particular account needs to be studied and embraced to learn what that particular moment offers.

Jesus is, for Christians, undoubtedly the most profound moment in God's story with the human family. What Jesus teaches over and over again is to recognize the depth of God's grace and the ever-so-wide circle of God's love. To walk in Jesus' way is to be strengthened by God's love and emboldened by God's Spirit to live and love as Jesus did. To find life and truth in Jesus is to celebrate God's most intimate and most particular sharing of divine love. But God is never restricted or limited by the particulars, only enhanced. Christians know Jesus to be the way to God. What we must not forget is that the God we meet in Jesus is the God whose love reaches out to all in relentless and diverse expressions of compassion, forgiveness, and re-creating love.

3

Finding the Life
Sharing along the Path

Chapter Eleven

Tell Me That Old New Story, Again

There is an old gospel song, still sung enthusiastically by some Christians, that goes, in part:

> Give me that old-time religion,
> Give me that old-time religion,
> Give me that old-time religion,
> And it's good enough for me.
> It was good for our mothers [fathers, martyrs, everybody, etc.; add
> your hero],
> It was good for our mothers
> It was good for our mothers,
> And it's good enough for me.

The song was first published in 1903 by Charles D. Tillman, but was the work of a now anonymous composer several decades earlier. It is marked by a catchy tune—almost anyone can get into the swing of it immediately—and a woefully uncritical nostalgia.

The "old-time religion" celebrated in this old song is hardly old by the standards of the history of Christianity, to say nothing about world history. It came out of the post–Civil War turmoil in the last half of the nineteenth century, a time of tremendous social upheaval and change. Implicitly, the song challenges the emerging modernism that in the first two decades of the twentieth century would be fought furiously by the leaders of fundamentalism, a battle still being waged in some Christian and non-Christian circles.

There were many facets in the struggle between modernism and fundamentalism, but much centered on how to read and interpret the Bible. The new biblical scholarship and the changing role of the church in relation to society were quite unsettling for many. Modern biblical scholarship was seen as questioning the authenticity of the biblical account, the very truth of God's Word. A simple religion that took the Bible simply and literally as God's direct word given once and for all without error ("inerrant" is the technical term), correctly translated only in the King James Version, was what many people wanted and what fundamentalism offered. These Christians wanted things to stay the same. They did not want, or trust, change. So they sang about that "old-time religion" to encourage one another and to draw a line in the sand, so to speak, about a religious stance they believed to be nonnegotiable.

For those who sing the song now, it seems to evoke a nostalgic wish for a kind of Norman Rockwell time when everyone looked the same (namely like me) and believed the right things (namely the things I believe) and went to church (and some, like me, of course, to the "right" church). Change is still viewed with great suspicion. Biblical scholarship is deeply mistrusted. "Pluralism" and "diversity" are considered as different aspects of a malicious attack against God. Of course, "back then," it is believed, was a time when none of these problems threatened average, normal Christians. Oh, indeed, give me that old-time religion! That such a time never actually existed is immaterial. Many think it did, and by singing loudly they are trying to bring it back in the midst of a world that has little place for such old-time religion.

Further, for many of these Christians the old-time religion is narrowly exclusive, indeed downright judgmental of anyone who does not profess Jesus in their very particular language. Somewhere along the way the song "Jesus *loves* me" became for many Christians "Jesus loves *me*." The song "Jesus loves the little children, all the children of the world" was altered by an interpretive perspective that changed the meaning to something like "Jesus loves the little children, all the children of the world, at least *all those who are like me and say the right words.*" Unfortunately, many if not most non-Christians have experienced a Christianity packaged in exactly such a form.

To put it another way, some Christians believe that the old-time religion praised in the catchy song—that religion that was good enough for Paul and Silas, for our mothers and our fathers, and countless others remembered in the endless verses—is the same as biblical faith. But that is simply not so. Indeed, what many Christians call the "*old* hymns" that encapsulate the "*old-time* religion" were in fact written between 1880 and 1920 CE, not very old and quite unrepresentative of the varied spectrum of biblical faith.

What is needed is a retelling of the story, a reconsideration of what old-time religion actually did look like, and the place to begin is the Bible. The story of the Bible, as considered in the preceding chapters, provides a rich narrative of "new things" brought by the Spirit of God. Across the panorama of the biblical canvas the circle of divine love is boldly displayed as wide and, for some, embarrassingly inclusive. All through the Old Testament (the Hebrew Bible, the First Testament), God is remembered as reaching out to all manner of persons in loving concern with the intention to rescue them, sometimes most especially from themselves. The New Testament (the Second Testament) continues the testimony about the wideness of God's love. Numerous biblical passages declare the far-reaching character of divine love. If we are to retell the story for the twenty-first century, the issue remains: How are we to read and interpret the Bible?

As has been repeatedly mentioned in the preceding chapters, the first principle to follow is that of context, context, context. There are several contexts that should be recognized and respected. In the first place, the Bible comes to the modern reader in translation. Ideally, each reader of the Bible should become sufficiently proficient in biblical Hebrew, Aramaic, and Greek in order to begin the task of reading and understanding. Of course, that is not practical, as helpful as it might be. So the next best course of action for most readers will be the use of multiple translations in whatever modern languages the reader does know. For instance, the Bible has been translated well in English, French, and Spanish, to name but a few. Acknowledging the ancient language context, and working to compensate for inaccessibility, is the first step.

Next, a second pair of contexts that need careful attention are those of the literary and historical settings of the different parts of the Bible. In order appropriately to read and interpret the Bible, to begin to appreciate the real old-time religion, readers have to recognize that actual human beings in very particular historical settings wrote the Bible. The authors, while certainly inspired by God's Holy Spirit, used the language and literary conventions of their own time. They utilized particular types of writing, ranging from psalm writing to narrative writing to letter writing and so on. A prophetic oracle should not be read in the same way as a legal statute. Each kind of literature has its own context.

Moreover, within each particular context verses should not be taken out of their literary context and heard separately as universal truths. The psalmist's affirmation, "the LORD is my shepherd, I shall not want" (Psalm 23:1), is metaphorical, not literal. The remainder of the psalm is required to give content to the image. This image can influence one's theology, but it is not a truth. Jesus' words, "I am the light of the world" (John 8:12), are metaphorical, not literal. These words are part of a particular passage that emphasizes the controversy surrounding discipleship to Jesus. The wider literary context in the Gospel of John, a Gospel in which Jesus' way is portrayed with a number of images, presents Jesus in a struggle between "light" and "darkness." This wider context enriches the picture of Jesus as a light in a dark world. It loses value when it is extracted from its context and presented as some form of absolute. For Christians, of course, the Bible includes not only the New Testament but the Old Testament as well, thereby expanding the literary context of every particular passage in either Testament.

The historical context, as has been noted repeatedly, is equally critical to recognize. In some instances precise dating of the biblical literature is not possible, but usually the general era can be identified if not the exact time. Any clues that can be found are important. It makes a big difference what was going on at the time something was written. An example from American history may help to make the point. Consider the following portion of a letter:

> Confidence of the whole union is centered in you. Your being at the helm will be more than an answer to every argument which can be used to alarm and lead the people in any quarter, into violence and secession. North and South will hang together if they have you to hang on; and if the first correction of a numerous representation

should fail in its effect, your presence will give time for trying others, not inconsistent with the union and peace of the states.

Now, what is this letter about? Most people, on first reading, jump on the words "North and South," "secession," and the "union and peace of the states" and assume that the historical setting is around the time of the Civil War. Such a guess makes some sense. But there are problems. To whom would this letter be written if the Civil War era were the setting? Abraham Lincoln? He was hardly a leader in whom the "whole union" had confidence. Indeed, he had political troubles within his own party. And what would "numerous representation" mean in a letter written around the time of the Civil War? To jump too quickly to an interpretation based on an assumed historical setting can be very misleading.

Actually, this is a portion of a letter written by Thomas Jefferson to George Washington in 1792 urging Washington to run for a second term in office. Though Jefferson did not really want Washington to have a second term—Jefferson was fearful that Washington might become a new "king"—he recognized that Washington was probably the only one who might be able to provide the stability that the new nation needed to survive the early tensions between North and South (among the original colonies) and allow time for the political process to work in uniting very different groups that had been made "one" by the war of independence against England.

I hope that this example indicates some of what is at stake in properly recognizing the historical context of any document or address or other literary construction. Jefferson's letter is capable of being misinterpreted badly if the correct setting is not determined. The same thing is true with respect to the Bible. An exact date may not always be possible, but broad dating usually is. That Paul wrote the letter to the Romans before the destruction of Jerusalem by the Romans in 70 CE is significant. The deep division within the Jewish community that eventually led to the emergence of Judaism and Christianity had not taken place when Paul wrote. Paul's letters have to be read in that light. To ignore the controversies within the Jewish community after 70 CE that provide the historical context for the Gospel of John can lead to disastrous misinterpretation of who Jesus is and what his followers are to believe and do. There are very good resources (Bible commentaries, Bible dictionaries, etc.) to assist readers of the Bible in recognizing and appreciating the numerous historical contexts reflected in the Bible, a collection of materials written over a span of at least one thousand years of history. Thoughtful, responsible readers will make use of such resources in the effort to recognize appropriate historical contexts as well as one can.

Yet another context is important, the context of the faith communities that preserved and passed along the Bible generation by generation down to the present. The Christian canon was made official in the last years of the fourth century CE, first by the Synod of Hippo in 393 and more authoritatively by the Synod of Carthage in 397. But unofficially the list of the books that were considered to belong rightly in the Bible was in wide use in the church by the beginning of the third century CE.

In the period that followed the destruction of Jerusalem in 70 CE the rabbinical leadership in the Jewish community began work on defining the Jewish canon, which was finalized somewhere between 90 and 110 CE. The list included all thirty-nine books that Protestant Christians have come to call the "Old Testament." Roman Catholic and Orthodox Christians have a slightly larger Old Testament because they follow what is known as the Alexandrian canon that had come into use among Greek-speaking Jews somewhere around 200 BCE. The Alexandrian canon is preserved in a Greek translation called the Septuagint. The rabbinical leaders, who authorized the official Hebrew canon around 100 CE, did not accept the Septuagint (largely because of its wide use among some Jewish sectarian groups that, by then, included the Christians). They chose instead a shorter Hebrew text that Protestant Christians adopted many centuries later.

The point of the above detour into the history of the text and the canon is this. For the first one hundred fifty years or so of the Common Era, the interpretation of the Bible was carried out in the historical context of a growing community awareness that ended in the separation of Jews and Christians. The New Testament represents part of the interpretation that was being done. The Bible (it was not yet called the "Old Testament") supplied the traditions upon which both Jews and Christians reflected as they tried to understand what God was doing in the history they were experiencing and what they in turn were called to do. For one hundred and fifty years increasing tension and animosity developed until, by 200 CE, a Christian theology and a Jewish theology were developing that defined each group over against the other as well as over against the surrounding culture in which both lived as clear minorities.

Emerging from this early historical period Christians stressed that they were equally, in every way, God's people along with the Jews. The church was God's way of creating a new relationship with all the non-Jewish people of the world, namely the Gentiles. Some Christians believed that God had rejected the Jews because they had not accepted Jesus, but this notion did not become commonly accepted until the beginning or middle of the third century CE. In the first two centuries of the Common Era, even with the clear differences that distinguished Christians and Jews, there were many more things that linked them—common scriptures, family and social traditions, patterns of worship, minority status in the Roman Empire.

This somewhat uneasy, but mutually accepting, relationship changed dramatically after the reign of Constantine (306–337 CE) when Christianity became the official religion of the Roman Empire. Christians suddenly constituted the vast majority within the society. Strong statements by earlier theologians and church leaders against Jews, primarily intended to provide identification and encouragement to the struggling Christian minority, took on a new tone when voiced by the new majority. Unflattering words and line-in-the-sand declarations meant something quite different when spoken between equals (as in this instance of Jews and Christians before Constantine). However, when one group, the Christians, became dominant and had the political power and encouragement to impose its views on the other, such statements had a different impact.

With the change in the balance of power there began a long history of hostility and repression, punctuated at various points with periods of overt persecution by Christians toward Jews. The long history of Christian scorn for and teaching against Jews culminated in the twentieth century when much Christian teaching was used by the Nazis in support of their intention to annihilate Jews and Judaism.

All of this is to emphasize how the context of the communities that have preserved and interpreted the Bible across the centuries clearly must be taken into consideration. The official theology, the rule of faith, of any particular group, particularly as reflected in creedal statements and instructional curricula, does affect interpretation, but theological positions change across the centuries. Thus from early in the history of the church another context was emphasized for the sake of balance, namely the Rule of Love.

Simply put, in light of the clear insistence in the Bible on God's love, a love that exercised both compassion and judgment, and the love manifest in the life and ministry of Jesus, all interpretation is to be exercised in the context of love. Teachings drawn from scripture and creed that are counter to divine love are suspect even when they may literally be supported by the tradition. The Rule of Love is not always easily employed, but it is a constant reminder that every historical and theological context stands within God's care and under divine sovereignty.

But now, back to that old-time religion. For over a thousand years—a very long time, to be sure—some Christians and Jews have understood the Bible in very exclusive ways. According to their understanding of the story, God cared only for them. Jews did not acknowledge Christians as having any relationship with the God celebrated as the God of Israel. The Christians who took the exclusive path believed Jews to have lost their special relation with God and to be no different from pagans, significant only as targets for proselytizing. The old-time religion of both groups, though clearly different, shared a very narrow understanding of God's intentions in the world.

This version of the old-time religion is now part of the contemporary context of interpretation. The Christian version of this narrow understanding of God's aim in the world is called "supersessionist" in that it understands the church to have taken the place of Israel in God's plan, to have "superseded" Judaism. This "our religion alone is best" attitude is what was earlier noted as feeding militant extremism so well in contemporary times. But because this interpretation of the biblical story has been around for so long, many people simply assume it must be right. It is difficult to get people to consider a new possibility.

To recognize a different point of view, however, is critical for at least two reasons. First, the Bible itself, as has been noted, clearly contradicts the narrow, supersessionist interpretation that God is concerned only with the chosen people, whether Jews or Christians. Second, if history is a reliable witness, such narrow approaches invariably produce much more hate than love. The historical and literary context of the Bible and the rule of love press for a retelling of the "old, old story of Jesus and his love."

Basic to the real old-time religion is the recognition that God's love never stops with the chosen people. Though there is a special relationship with the bearers of the story, both Jews and Christians, the divine love extends far beyond both. The story of the Bible is an account of the numerous ways God extends and demonstrates love to countless people. God's love is made quite particular in the context of human history—specific people in specific moments—but that love is never limited to or controlled by those who receive it or announce it. From Noah to Abraham and Sarah to Isaiah, Jonah, and Ruth and on to Jesus and his followers, God is remembered as seeking all manner of peoples with whom to engage in a loving, redeeming relationship.

To put it another way, the old-time religion of the Bible is not about "us and them." It is about God—a gracious, loving, all-embracing God, who regularly surprises the human family with a generosity of love beyond our imagination. The prophet writing from the midst of the despair of exile summed up this experience of God well with these words:

> Seek the LORD while he may be found,
>   call upon him while he is near;
> let the wicked forsake their way,
>   and the unrighteous their thoughts;
> let them return to the LORD, that he may have mercy on them,
>   and to our God, for he will abundantly pardon.
> For my thoughts are not your thoughts,
>   nor are your ways my ways, says the LORD.
> For as the heavens are higher than the earth,
>   so are my ways higher than your ways
>   and my thoughts than your thoughts.
>
> Isaiah 55:6–9

The story that the Bible tells is of a divine love almost incomprehensibly wide, extended to all, excluding no one. God's love powered the creation of all that is and continues to shape the world and those that inhabit it. The Bible is quick to point out that humans do not regularly respond to God's wondrous love in ways pleasing to God, but that does not limit or destroy that love. The real old-time religion is about that love, and it challenges our prejudices and fears by inviting us to risk all—especially any sense of privilege before God—for the sake of that love.

Chapter Twelve

What Difference Does "Belief" Make?

*I*n his best-selling action mystery, *The Da Vinci Code,* author Dan Brown recounts this exchange between his two principal characters:

> Langdon smiled: "Sophie, *every* faith in the world is based on fabrication. That is the definition of *faith*—acceptance of that which we imagine to be true, that which we cannot prove. Every religion describes God through metaphor, allegory, and exaggeration, from the early Egyptians through modern Sunday school. Metaphors are a way to help our minds process the unprocessible. The problems arise when we begin to believe literally in our own metaphors." (Brown 2003, 341–42)

Whether one agrees with Langdon's view, he makes a critical point. Problems arise when the character and purpose of belief are disregarded or misunderstood.

An example from the history of the Christian movement will perhaps help to illustrate this point. In 325 CE Emperor Constantine, who had only the year before become the undisputed head of the Roman Empire, convened a gathering of bishops. The meeting was held in Nicaea, a city located about sixty miles from modern-day Istanbul in northwest Turkey. Constantine had a very political reason for bringing the bishops together. He wanted them to settle a theological controversy that was proving quite divisive across the empire that he had been working diligently to unite for well over a decade.

There is no way of knowing just how much the content of the theological debate actually mattered to the emperor. He was not officially a Christian yet—he did not receive baptism until immediately before his death in 337 CE. But, following a miraculous military victory in 313 CE (at which time, by virtue of a vision Constantine had had, his troops wore a cross on their uniforms evoking the help of the Christian God), Constantine had shown high regard for and offered protection to the Christians in the empire. What is clear is that the strongly held beliefs among the competing Christian theologians were having destabilizing effects within the empire, and Constantine wanted to put an end to the controversy. Thus he convened what has come to be known in church history as the Council of Nicaea.

The issue centered on the teaching of a priest named Arius (ca. 250–336 CE), who lived near Alexandria, Egypt. The fundamental issue revolved around how to express the relationship of the Lord Jesus with the one and only God revered in the First (Old) Testament and by the early church. Was Jesus divine or not? If so, what did that do to the monotheism, the belief that there was but one God, that was such a distinctive mark of Judaism and the early Christian movement? Both Jews and Christians were labeled "atheists" early on because, on the basis of their monotheistic convictions, they refused to acknowledge the pantheon of deities honored around the Roman Empire, and especially they rejected the deification and worship of the emperors.

Arius contended that Jesus, as a man, was necessarily subordinate to God. Because he was a human, Jesus was limited in his knowledge, bound by the flesh. Jesus had a more perfect relationship with God than all other women and men, but he was nonetheless a creature, and thereby subject, not equal, to God. Jesus was to be understood as "Son of God," Arius believed, because God had "adopted" Jesus as a "son." But what was most important was that Jesus shared essentially in the humanity of all other human beings. In arguing his position, Arius pointed out that Jesus repeatedly found it important to pray to God, whom he called "Abba," Father. Jesus ate and slept, cried and got angry, and eventually was crucified and died. All of these facts supported Arius's understanding of Jesus and of Jesus' subordination before God.

But if Arius's view was persuasive to some, it was considered dangerously wrong by others, and thus Constantine gathered the bishops. Among the more outspoken opponents, and one of the most articulate, was Athanasius, who at the time of the council was an assistant to Bishop Alexander of Alexandria. Three years later, in 328 CE, following Alexander's death, Athanasius himself became bishop and had an even stronger position of power from which to continue his denunciation of Arius's views.

For Athanasius the deity of Jesus was at stake. He insisted that Jesus was much more than just a human. Jesus, according to Athanasius, shared in the very substance of God. He insisted that Jesus' authority rested in the fact that, though human, he was also divine. The "Son of God" language used in reference to Jesus required, in Athanasius's view, that Jesus be understood as of "one being" with God the Father. The identification of Jesus with God was not accidental. It was metaphysical.

Though the Council of Nicaea overwhelmingly endorsed Athanasius's position over that of Arius, many years of controversy and turmoil followed. Numerous bishops, magistrates, and even emperors continued to support Arius's position. Conflict, actual physical conflict, and at times oppression occurred between the debating parties. Belief led to division and animosity. Eventually, some fifty years later, the dust settled, and Athanasius's view prevailed. A baptismal creed, now known as the Nicene Creed, was adopted at another council, the Council of Constantinople, 381 CE, solidifying the theological affirmations considered crucial by Athanasius.

One outcome of this great dispute was the clear emergence of an orthodoxy over against which people and positions could be judged. In the early decades of the Christian movement diversity, not uniformity, was the norm. Toward the end of the second century of the Common Era, however, a trend had begun with selected theological statements, as well as selected biblical documents, becoming more normative and more and more important if one wanted to be a true Christian.

This trend came in response to a variety of new views that were springing up, some of which came to be labeled "gnostic," that seemed to diverge rather dramatically from the earliest traditions. To some church leaders it seemed that too many believers were being led away from the core tradition. Doctrinal purity became more and more important. This trend toward establishing a normative orthodoxy culminated with the Councils of Nicaea and Constantinople. After these councils, heresy was definable and was to be rooted out. The church, aided by the power and authority of the empire, initiated an era in which the church determined what was correct belief and punished those who veered from the norm.

Whether the Arian controversy occurred because metaphors were violated by literal interpretation or because the metaphors required the clarification brought by keener insight is still debated. The point here is not to resolve the dispute. Rather, this is but an example of how beliefs can and have affected deeply the way people order their lives and relate to or separate from others. On the basis of these "beliefs" political decisions were made that had an impact on vast numbers of people, then and now.

Sometimes many generations later beliefs can be and are claimed in support of positions quite removed from the original setting of dispute. In an important book titled *Has God Only One Blessing?* Mary C. Boys has explored the relationship of Christianity with Judaism. At one point in her study, she reflects on the Arius-Athanasius conflict. She draws attention to a very troubling theme in Athanasius's argument, a disturbingly modern anti-Jewish disposition used as a subtext by Athanasius. Part of Athanasius's argument against Arius's contention that Jesus was human, sharing only by adoption in God's divinity, was the assertion that Arius in his reasoning was being "just like the Jews" in their rejection of Jesus. Boys quotes Athanasius as follows:

> Since this sort of madness is a Jewish thing, and Jewish in the way that Judas the traitor was Jewish, let them [the Arians] profess openly that they are disciples of Caiphas and Herod and stop disguising Judaism with the name of Christianity. . . . Or else, if they fear to be openly Jewish and to be circumcised because they do not want to displease Constantius [son of Constantine who ruled the Eastern empire 337–361] and the people they have led astray, let them stop saying what the Jews said, for it is only fair to turn away from the opinions of those whose name they reject. . . . If you too want to become Christians, rid yourselves of Arius's madness and cleanse with the language of piety that hearing of yours which blasphemy has soiled. Know that when you cease being Arians you will also cease from the folly of the Jews, and that truth will immediately illumine you like light shining out of darkness. (Boys 2000, 168)

Boys's observation is particularly troubling because it demonstrates just how long anti-Jewish animosity has been at work in the church and accepted as truth because some influential and respected theologians endorsed it. Beliefs are very important, but they can be destructive. Across the centuries a theological dispute that seems rather philosophical and removed from where most people live today has the power to erupt in extremely harmful behavior by Christians against Jews, and sometimes against Muslims as well, justified in the name of protecting Jesus from being defamed.

So what shall we do? Suspend belief? No, that is hardly possible or advisable. It is not possible because even the contention that "I don't believe" is a belief. Some people like to think that they have no beliefs, but what they actually mean is that they do not hold particular beliefs. Indeed, they may be able to list a set of things that they do not believe. What may be important for them to do is to list what they actually do believe, because all of us have beliefs.

It is quite misleading when people think they have no beliefs, for such a stance is simply impossible. And it is unwise to recommend to people that they should have no beliefs because, first, it is not possible, and second, almost universally such a stance grants permission for ignorance and denial. Some of the most troubling beliefs, so far as the common good is concerned, are unacknowledged beliefs that deeply influence behavior. Depending upon whether one agrees with them, such beliefs can be called "values" or "prejudices."

What makes them troublesome is that they often underlie behavior without even being recognized. Unarticulated beliefs cannot be tested or corrected. Many Christians (and, of course, adherents of other religions as well) are guided by beliefs that they have not actually examined, beliefs that they may not consciously even know they hold. That presents a difficult and dangerous situation for those who want religious belief to provide a positive guide for individual behavior that not only is personally pleasing but also enhances the common good.

About a decade ago a movement began (mostly in evangelical circles) to urge people to wear wristbands, buttons, and other items of clothing or decoration that were emblazoned with "WWJD?" The coded message was a reminder to the wearer whenever in situations that required ethical decision to pause and ask, "What Would Jesus Do?" The practice can be faulted in various ways, not the least being that there is simply no way to know what Jesus might do in a world so vastly different from that of the first century. But the notion that some point of measure is needed to help shape beliefs that thereby can guide one through the complexities of life is on target.

Indeed, Christians have employed a number of "WWJD?" symbols across the centuries for just that reason. The formal name given to this centuries-old practice is to follow the Rule of Faith, which consists of a basic summary of the official, creedal theology at any given time in history. The content of that rule has changed from generation to generation depending upon the issues that the faithful were facing, but the appeal to belief beyond the merely individual level has not. Individuals have always needed the guidance of wider communities, even individuals who rebelled against or resisted the very communities that nurtured them.

The Rule of Faith is a reminder that there is always a past to the current present, and there will most likely be a future as well. Each of us as we fashion our beliefs do so in that ongoing stream of history. We inherit much of our belief system from those into whose lives we are born. Families, congregations, towns, nations, and a myriad of other groups through which we pass help shape our beliefs. For intentional Christians, those Christians who are seriously trying to live according to their faith, the guidance of the church is of great importance. Thus, knowingly or unknowingly, they turn to the Rule of Faith for guidance.

As already mentioned, the content of the Rule of Faith is not eternally fixed. But across the centuries there is some continuity. Creedal statements such as those noted at the beginning of this chapter exercise ongoing guidance. New creeds emerge, and if they prove useful, they are passed along as testimony from one generation to succeeding generations. There are clearly major themes that are repeatedly affirmed about the character of God and the continuing work of God by the power of the divine Spirit. But the challenges before the church, and those engaging individual Christians, at any particular time may require that certain traditional beliefs be claimed as more— or less—important in light of the circumstances faced. The Holy

Spirit may in fact bring new insight that shapes response in a way different from the way previous generations of believers have dealt with an issue. Still, the Rule of Faith is the reminder that individual Christians must always test their beliefs over against the wider religious tradition of which they are a part.

Another guideline can and should be involved in this belief-shaping business, namely the Rule of Love. I mentioned it at the end of the previous chapter. The basic conviction behind this guideline is that the Bible insists on a twofold commandment intended to give humans direction in life, namely that we are to love God and love neighbor. Any belief that causes one to violate either part of this twofold Rule of Love should be viewed with suspicion as inadequate, mistaken, or perverse.

The Rule of Love requires a regular review of premises and presumptions, of how what we say we believe actually affects the way we live. Belief is second to love according to this rubric, not the other way around. What Jesus did do was to reach out to all manner of folk and extend to them the love of God. This love was the truth and life of the way he called his disciples to follow.

Jesus disregarded traditional belief barriers associated with sex, status, and sickness. He knew that people believed lepers to be unclean and untouchable, but he reached out anyway and touched a leper and extended healing (Luke 5:12–14). Jesus knew that common opinion held tax collectors to be unworthy of inclusion, indeed worthy of exclusion, but he called Levi anyway making him one of the twelve apostles (5:27–39). Jesus knew what people believed about men and women talking together in public, but he allowed a woman, "a sinner," to touch him in public anyway, "kissing his feet and anointing them with ointment." When criticized, Jesus pronounced forgiveness for the woman and commended her great love (7:36–50). Belief certainly has a place, but for Jesus at least, the Rule of Love was paramount.

So if beliefs are unavoidable and are influential, what can be done at the practical level to fashion good beliefs? First, it is important to distinguish between fact and fiction. Some beliefs are based on error or falsehood. For instance, a generation ago children (and adults for that matter) were advised not to go swimming for at least thirty minutes after having eaten. Whatever good this conviction might have accomplished, it was untrue. There is simply no scientific reason to wait. Or again, millions of people lived and died believing that the sun rose in the morning and set each night circling the earth that clearly stood at the center of the universe. Though believed unquestionably by practically everyone for centuries, and despite its reasonableness on the basis of everyday experience, this belief was simply untrue.

Now some beliefs that are demonstrably untrue bring little negative consequence. Whether the sun circles the earth or the earth the sun does not matter, in one sense, in terms of how daily life is conducted. But left unchallenged, other beliefs based on incorrect data or data created as pure falsehood spark exceedingly bad behavior. For instance, a document titled "The Protocols of the Learned Elders of Zion" has long been recognized as anti-Jewish propaganda. It is absolutely false. Nonetheless, people continue to circulate it in the Middle East (very recently a "documentary" based on the "Protocols" was run on the state-controlled television station in Egypt) to stir up mistrust and hatred. The "Protocols" are uncritically accepted as true and shape the beliefs of some hate groups in North America and Europe as well. Beliefs based on this spurious document are certainly divisive and potentially dangerous.

Beyond determining the difference between fact and falsehood, however, is a second factor important to consider. Some beliefs are rightly based on data that are not factual in the empirical sense of that term, but not fictional in the usual sense of that term either. The stories in the early chapters of Genesis, for instance, are not historically true, but symbolically they are quite true. Such stories have a mythic quality that invites the human reader/hearer to identify with and reflect on the truthfulness of the accounts without the need to literalize them. They are accounts intended to share a basic understanding of reality with the intention of drawing the believer into an acceptance of that world with its values.

In the same way, there is a whole set of stories about the founders of the United States. Some of these stories are factually, historically true, like the accounts of the framing of the Constitution. Others, however, are not literally true but, nonetheless, do rightly uphold some aspect of the national values, such as the story of George Washington and the cherry tree. If telling the truth were not held in such high regard, the critics of recent presidents would not receive much of a hearing. The truth of Washington exceeds the particulars of some of the stories and fosters belief that remains warranted.

This brings us to the final point about belief. The task that is critical is to be aware of what one believes and why, and then to test these beliefs to see if they are worthy of the guidance they are exercising. This is not a task that can be done alone. Few, if any, can be so self-critical and self-discerning as to be able to sort out the character and purpose of one's own beliefs. Further, few of the beliefs that really matter are solely or mainly individual. Racial prejudice, for instance, is almost always a collective, societal creation. So it is important to find places where beliefs and their consequences can be honestly examined, no easy enterprise.

Humans seem inherently to form beliefs. Thus it is not credible to suggest simply not having any beliefs lest the ones we have turn out to be incorrect or lead to bad behavior. What is necessary is a willingness to update one's beliefs in light of new information, including new experience. The enemy is the temptation, as Langdon told Sophie, to begin to believe literally in our own metaphors

Jonathan Sacks in *The Dignity of Difference* addresses a somewhat related issue in this way:

> Truth on earth is not, nor can it aspire to be, the whole truth. It is limited, not comprehensive; particular, not universal. When two propositions conflict it is not necessarily because one is true the other false. It may be, and often is, that each represents a different perspective on reality. . . . In heaven there is truth, on earth there are truths. . . . The wisest is not one who knows himself wiser than others: he is one who knows all men have some share of the truth, and is willing to learn from them, for none of us knows all the truth and each of us knows some of it. (Sacks 2002, 64–65)

We do not live without beliefs. But we should not live informed by unexamined, untested, merely assumed beliefs. Responsibly developing and living intentionally by our beliefs is the challenge.

Chapter Thirteen

We Really Do Need to Talk— with Others!

*I*n the preface to her award-winning book *Encountering God: A Spiritual Journey from Bozeman to Banaras*, Diana Eck has written:

> The Indian philosopher Krishnamurti has said, "Relationship is the mirror in which we see ourselves as we really are." This is especially true in our relationships with people of other religious traditions. In the give and take of dialogue, understanding one another leads to mutual self-understanding and finally to mutual transformation. My encounter with Hindus has enabled me to understand my own faith more clearly and has required that I understand my own faith differently. It would only be honest to say that my faith as a Christian has been shaped by several religious traditions. (Eck 1993, xii)

Does one really need to talk with others about what one believes and what one considers the essential values in life to be? Perhaps not, if one is perfectly content with things as they are, if one sees no need for or room for change, if deeper insight holds no attraction or appeal. Dialogue is without purpose if one really knows all there is to know.

Experience suggests, however, that few, if any, have attained such a mastery of life. What's more, the wisest among us urge us to talk with one another, to listen to one another, to share and learn from one another. The testimony of persons like Diana Eck, for one, is that it is in dialogue that we best come to know not only what others believe but what we believe as well, and why we think it is important. In thoughtful conversation with others we come to see how our truth relates to all the other truths held by those of different backgrounds and experiences. Do we need to talk with others? Yes, if we want to be what God intends us to be. And that talking needs to take at least two forms.

So where does one begin? The first challenge is to recognize the profound difference that exists between who God actually is in contrast to how any particular group of human beings (including my own) tries to describe who God is. In the preceding chapters I have repeatedly mentioned that divine love extends far beyond what is often assumed or believed. Despite the numerous clues the Bible offers to this reality, many still believe otherwise and claim that God loves only them or their group. Diversity is seen as a threat rather than a gift. Many seem to assume that other people—and their understandings—exist solely for the purpose of conversion or eradication. One's understanding of God and God's purposes is critical in defining one's stance toward others.

Some fifty years ago, in a quite different era, J. B. Phillips wrote a profound book addressed to this very problem of underestimating God. The issues that prompted Phillips to write are not the same, for the most part, as those we wrestle with today, but the attitude that creates a problem is not all that different. Phillips's book led many readers to a healthy reexamination of their faith. The book was titled *Your God Is Too Small*. In his "Introductory" Phillips wrote:

> Many men and women today are living, often with inner dissatisfaction, without any faith in God at all. This is not because they are particularly wicked or selfish or, as the old-fashioned would say, "godless," but because they have not found with their adult minds a God big enough to "account for" life, big enough to "fit in with" the new scientific age, big enough to command their highest admiration and respect, and consequently their willing co-operation. (Phillips 1953, vi)

For the current generation part of that "smallness" resides in the unexplored assumption of a divine narrowness that is not at all biblical. Many loud voices claim a divine exclusiveness that, if true, would make dialogue with others unnecessary and perhaps even unwise. Nonetheless, there are others, including clear voices within the Bible, that urge a reconsideration of the narrowness assumption and an open engagement with others who believe differently, within Christianity and beyond.

More recently Rabbi Jonathan Sacks has addressed the same point from this angle:

> The same applies to religion. The radical transcendence of God in the Hebrew Bible means nothing more or less than that *there is a difference between God and religion.* God is universal, religions are particular. Religion is the translation of God into a particular language and thus into the life of a group, a nation, a community of faith. In the course of history, God has spoken to mankind in many languages: through Judaism to Jews, Christianity to Christians, Islam to Muslims. Only such a God is truly transcendental—greater not only than the natural universe but also than the spiritual universe articulated in any single faith, any specific language of human sensibility. How could a sacred text convey such an idea? It would declare that *God is God of all humanity, but no single faith is or should be the faith of all humanity.* Only such a narrative would lead us to see the presence of God in people of other faiths. Only such a worldview could reconcile the particularity of cultures with the universality of the human condition. (Sacks 2002, 55)

Using the "exclusivist," "inclusivist," "pluralist" distinctions mentioned earlier in chapter three, and aiming to underscore the need for dialogue, Diana Eck has written:

> If the move toward pluralism begins theologically in the places where people of different traditions find an openness—and even an imperative—toward encounter with one another, it begins historically and culturally with the plain fact of our religious diversity, our cultural proximity to one another, and our human interdependence. In very practical terms, how are we all to live with one another in a climate of mutuality and understanding? Is it even possible? Those who live according to an exclusivist paradigm frankly do not wish to live closely with people of other faiths and would prefer to shut them out—which is increasingly impossible—or to convert others to their own view of the world. Those who appropriate differences, as do the inclusivists, assume that the worldview of others looks very much like their own, and the ground rules are presumed to be "ours." But those who think about life together as pluralists recognize the need for radical new forms of living together and communicating with one another. (Eck 1993, 191)

And further:

If our world were a village of a thousand people, who would *we* be? The World Development Forum tells us that there would be 329 Christians, 174 Muslims, 131 Hindus, 61 Buddhists, 52 Animists, 3 Jews, 34 members of other religions, such as Sikhs, Jains, Zoroastrians, and Baha'is, and 216 would be without any religion. In this village, there would be 564 Asians, 210 Europeans, 86 Africans, 80 South Americans, and 60 North Americans. And in this same village, 60 persons would have half the income, 500 would be hungry, 600 would live in shantytowns, and 700 would be illiterate. (Eck 1993, 202)

In such a world the need for mutual understanding, and mutual transformation, is critical. Dialogue, not military or economic domination, seems to offer the best way to develop the kind of community that can support and enable all of us, with our great diversities, to live together and build a just society that will benefit all. Dialogue does not mean simply hanging out and gabbing. Dialogue requires serious commitment and energy.

To dialogue with another individual or group it is first imperative to know what one's own convictions are. To be sure, I may change my opinions, and even my beliefs, in the course of trying to share them with others, but if I do not believe anything, then I do not have any reason for or basis for entering into serious discussion with anyone else. Dialogue does not begin with the assumption that every opinion or idea is equally correct or valuable. Rather, dialogue begins with the conviction that what I believe is true and worth sharing with others. But serious conversation with others equally assumes that what they believe about life is worth hearing. Their beliefs provide a reality over against which to explore my own convictions and commitments, clarifying and adjusting in light of deepened insight.

There is a parable, offered in conversation between Jonathan Sacks and the leader of a very exclusive Jewish group, who rather unexpectedly underscored this very need to listen to others:

Imagine, he said, two people who spend their lives transporting stones. One carries bags of diamonds. The other hauls sacks of rocks. Each is now asked to take a consignment of rubies. Which of the two understands what he is now to carry? The man who is used to diamonds knows that stones can be precious, even those that are not diamonds. But the man who has carried only rocks thinks of stones as a mere burden. They have weight but not worth. Rubies are beyond his comprehension.

So it is, he said, with faith. If we cherish our own, then we will understand the value of others. We may regard ours as a diamond and another faith as a ruby, but we know that both are precious stones. But if faith is a mere burden, not only will we not value ours. Neither will we value the faith of someone else. We will see both as equally useless. True tolerance, he implied, comes not from the absence of faith but from its living presence. Understanding the particularity of what matters to us is the best way of coming to appreciate what matters to others. (Sacks 2002, 208–9)

For most of us, clarity requires study and discussion, first within our own group and only later with those of other traditions. Sometimes, though, it is helpful to have persons from outside our group to pose questions and to register reactions. It is important to realize that many Jews and Muslims, for instance, have serious misgivings about whether Christians actually worship one God or three. We need to struggle with our own understanding of the Trinity before we try to explain the doctrine to others. Questions from outsiders can help direct our search for self-understanding as we seek to decide what is truly important and what is merely custom. The aim is to prepare for discussion with others not so much to disqualify various opinions as to recognize the greater truth witnessed by and maintained in our rich diversity.

In modern society there are no simple answers to serious questions. People of goodwill can and will disagree about proposed solutions. But we desire and need to find ways to live together, acknowledging our differences while striving genuinely to appreciate the contributions each of us brings. Sustained engagement, perhaps in the form of structured conversation, may provide the avenue. It is important to discover how others perceive us, how they hear what we are trying to say. People of other faiths have sincere questions to pose, but there are few contexts that allow honest inquiry. If we want to better understand ourselves and contribute to a richer appreciation of the common diversity in which we live, we need to seek out such opportunities for conversation or intentionally set some up. They do not just happen, but they are critical in the effort to provide alternatives to the misinterpreted religious messages feeding militant extremism.

The issue is not who is right and who is wrong. Debate is not the mode. Growing awareness of one's own questions and one's own inadequacies in providing answers for both self and others is the goal. In the midst of open discussion and honest exploration some changes will probably take place, in oneself as well as in one's conversation partners, but that is only a by-product of openness, not the goal. Diversity is a reality and from the biblical perspective a valuable gift of God's love. To discover how I fit in with others also created by God is important and strenuous work.

So the first kind of talking that Christians need to do has to do with clarifying our own understanding of who God is and who we are. A critical part of this conversation should be with persons of other faiths. It is not enough, however, to converse only at the individual, coffee-break level. Tolerance is certainly well learned and exercised in this way, but a deeper encounter is necessary to broaden our basic assumptions and understandings about God and life. Disciplined study and conversation with others is what is needed. Coming to know God is foundational; coming to understand God is what the rest of the story is about.

That brings us to the second kind of talking that Christians must do with others. Witnessing to the love of God in Jesus Christ has always been a primary task of Christian discipleship. Having received forgiveness through Jesus Christ, Christians are to proclaim the good news of divine forgiveness to others. Having glimpsed the vision of God's just and healing reign, Christians are sent out to announce this good news and invite others to join in celebrating, demonstrating, and awaiting the fullness of God's loving purpose to be realized in all the world.

This kind of talking with others has traditionally been called "evangelism." It is not the work of professionals, though some professional evangelists do exist. It does not require polished public-speaking skills, though such abilities never hurt. It can be done in large or small groups, though most effective, in the long run, are one-on-one encounters with neighbors, colleagues at work or school, friends, and sometimes even strangers. It does not require a completely worked-out theological understanding of all the doctrines of the church (even if that were possible), though the claim of ignorance has often been put forward as an excuse for doing nothing. What Christian evangelism does require is a willingness to tell others of the extraordinary love God has shown in Jesus Christ along with an invitation to join in the work of the church as it strives to make concrete God's way in the world.

There are, however, at least two inhibitors for this kind of God-talk in the minds of many. First, for many North Americans, religion has come to be understood as strictly a private matter. My own individual beliefs are nobody else's business. I do not tell you what you should believe because I do not want you telling me what you think I should believe. In a broad way—and certainly as perceived by those who stand outside the church—Christians believe the same basic things, but in a myriad of particular ways they interpret the core tradition quite differently. To avoid conflict, it is easier just not to talk about what really matters to us individually or personally.

Add to this privatization of faith the fact that contemporary North American culture has little room for a transcendent God anyway, and especially one who requires moral commitments on the part of human beings. For the most part, at the practical level of the everyday chores, God is simply not needed. So why should one talk about God? Probably one will be considered, by others, as just a little weird if one does.

The second inhibitor working against participation in evangelism is of a different sort. It stems from negative experiences at the hands or mouths of some overly aggressive Christians who believe that their job is to save others. When challenged, they will hasten to say that God does the saving, not them, but their methods and techniques belie their protestations. They act as if they firmly believed that the end justifies the means and therefore anything goes in trying to get someone to profess faith in Jesus. The techniques range from overzealous efforts at trying to make people feel guilty to what many would call "brainwashing." Those of other faith traditions resent deeply these proselytizing efforts. Furthermore, other Christians who do not share this understanding of evangelism do not like it either when they or their children become the objects of attack by these "we're saved and you aren't" zealots.

Despite the fact that talking about God is not especially fashionable and that some people are downright obnoxious about it when they do it, we still do need to talk with others about God for at least three reasons. First and foremost, our primary task is to witness to the glory and grace of our God. Christians have been saved for service. That service involves speaking on God's behalf by literal word of mouth and by acts of justice and mercy. Christians are sent into the world to bring light and instruction to the peoples of the world. Contrary to much popular opinion, this does not require that Christians try to make everyone else become a Christian. Rather, the insistence is that, like salt, the message Christians are commissioned to announce is important for the well-being of the wider human community.

God created the church, among other reasons, as a demonstration classroom to present over and over again the drama of human sin and divine forgiveness. People from every nation, from every ethnic and racial background, both male and female, from all economic strata have been called into service in the church with the primary charge to love one another. The task is, by example, to display the love of God that has brought us together, a love capable of bridging everything that tends to divide and separate us from one another. How we talk—or don't talk—with each other as we try to resolve internal conflicts in the church is important, and, we should remember, it is at the same time one way we talk to those outside the church. This kind of speaking by word and deed is demanding and inescapable. This is the assignment given to those who become Christians. The only issue is how well we will carry it out.

The second reason we need to talk with others is to share the biblical message of the wideness of divine love. As already noted, too many people have the idea that God's love is limited only to a few when in fact divine love extends to all. We need to articulate a clearer understanding of the character of God and of God's intention for justice and kindness to reach to all. Sometimes we defame God by assuming limitations on God's love that the Bible certainly does not affirm. God does not belong to us—any of us! We belong to God—all of us! From the beginning of the story God has reached out to the whole human family both in judgment and with forgiveness. By working through particular individuals and peoples, God has repeatedly demonstrated the intention to enrich and embrace all people. At the end of the biblical story in Revelation 22:3 the tree of life is celebrated and its leaves recognized as intended "for the healing of the nations."

Since at least the time of Constantine, too many Christians have equated the boundaries of divine love with the boundaries of the church. Nothing could be further from the biblical perception or from the experience of a multitude of believers. Yes, God loves those within the church, but God also loves those not in the church. What then, some will ask, is the advantage of being a Christian? None, except having a God-given license to love one another freely and with abandon, and to talk about it.

The third reason why it is especially important for Christians to talk with others these days is the state of the world in which we live. Though it is only one ingredient in the social/political complex out of which decisions are made, religion is important. How one understands God can be decisive in how one relates to others. If you take the "God is on our side no matter what" position, a particular set of responses will be made to the people and problems of the world. Quite a different set of actions is drawn forth by the understanding that God forgives even the worst of enemies. Thus it is important to share the biblical witness to a divine love that is incredibly wide in its reach.

Near the conclusion of his book *The Dignity of Difference* Jonathan Sacks makes this important observation:

> I believe that we can no longer, as religious leaders, assume that nothing has changed in the human situation. Something *has* changed: our power for good and evil, the sheer reach and consequences of our interventions. We have come face to face with the stranger, and it makes all the difference whether we find this threatening or enlarging. Every great faith has within it harsh texts which, read literally, can be taken to endorse narrow particularism,

suspicion of strangers, and intolerance toward those who believe differently than we do. Every great faith also has within it sources that emphasize kinship with the stranger, empathy with the outsider, the courage that leads people to extend a hand across boundaries of estrangement or hostility. The choice is ours. Will the generous texts of our traditions serve as interpretative keys to the rest, or will the abrasive passages determine our ideas of what we are and what we are called on to do? No tradition is free from the constant need to reinterpret, to apply eternal truths to an ever-changing world, to listen to what God's word requires of me, here, now. That is what religious leaders have always done, in the past no less than now. (Sacks 2002, 207–8)

The "generous texts" are so important! That is what this book has tried to highlight. God can be pictured as a little god of clan or tribe or nation, or in our age, a god who cares just for me, the solitary individual, the only one who counts. But the wider biblical characterization of the Divine is so much richer. Creator, ruler of nations, protector of freedom and justice, source of human wisdom, open to all and inviting to all—that is the way God is portrayed in the Bible. Indeed, Jesus does embody the very way of living truth and came into our midst to demonstrate that way for us. It is a gracious way, a loving way, an affirming way, that can be shared with all. Therein lies its truth.

Reference List

Boys, Mary C. 2000. *Has God Only One Blessing?* New York: Paulist Press.

Brown, Dan. 2003. *The Da Vinci Code.* New York: Doubleday.

Confucius. "The Sayings of Confucius." *Harvard Classics.* Vol. 44, part 1. New York: P. F. Collier & Son, 1910.

Eck, Diana. 1993. *Encountering God: A Spiritual Journey from Bozeman to Banaras.* Boston: Beacon.

Feiler, Bruce. 2002. *Abraham: A Journey to the Heart of Three Faiths.* San Francisco: HarperCollins.

Friedman, Thomas L. 2002. *Longitudes and Attitudes: Exploring the World after September 11.* New York: Farrar, Straus & Giroux.

Newsom, Carol A. 1996. "The Book of Job." Pages 317–634 in *The New Interpreter's Bible.* Vol. 4, ed. Leander E. Keck. Nashville: Abingdon.

O'Day, Gail R. 1995. "The Gospel of John." Pages 491–865 in *The New Interpreter's Bible.* Vol. 9, ed. Leander E. Keck. Nashville: Abingdon.

Phillips, J. B. 1953. *Your God Is Too Small.* New York: Macmillan.

Pritchard, James B. 1969. *Ancient Near Eastern Texts Relating to the Old Testament.* 3d ed. Princeton: Princeton Univ. Press.

Sacks, Jonathan. 2002. *The Dignity of Difference.* London and New York: Continuum.